SEO 2015
Learn Search Engine Optimization with Smart Internet Marketing Strategies

Adam Clarke

Digital Book Guru, Publisher.
Cover Design: Digital Book Guru.
Production and Composition: Digital Book Guru.

SEO 2015: Learn search engine optimization with smart internet marketing strategies
Adam Clarke
Kindle ASIN B00NH0XZR0
Print ISBN-10: 1505578868
Print ISBN-13: 978-1505578867

Table of Contents

4

Introduction

So you've picked up SEO 2015 and decided to learn search engine optimization. Congratulations. SEO marketing can change your life.

Over 10-years ago I achieved my first number one ranking in Google for my family's accounting business. The phone started ringing with new customers every day. I was hooked.

Since then, I have used search engine optimization to grow small family-owned businesses, sex toy stores, large international fashion brands, and hotel chains. I have grown small businesses into giant companies in just one or two years — simply from working the client's website up to the top position in Google.

One thing never ceases to amaze me — SEO is the most powerful internet marketing tool to grow any business.

Unfortunately, learning how to use SEO is difficult, if not impossible, for most business owners, marketers and even tech-heads.

I have a theory on why this is so...

Sifting through the amount of information flooding the Internet about SEO is overwhelming. In many cases, the advice published is either outdated or misleading.

And the constant updates by Google make it even harder for SEO beginners and gurus alike to keep up with what works.

SEO can be simple and used by absolutely anyone to rank at the top of Google, grow their business and make money online.

It's a matter of having up-to-date information on how Google works, using the techniques that are most effective and taking action.

Whether you're a complete SEO newbie or well-versed internet marketing veteran, SEO 2015 covers these areas and sets out to make it as straightforward as possible to achieve more rankings, traffic and sales in 2015.

Enjoy.

Introduction to how Google works.

You can feel like a dog chasing its own tail trying to figure out how Google works.

There are thousands of bloggers and journalists spreading volumes of information that simply isn't true. If you follow all of the advice about SEO written on blogs, it's not only unlikely you will receive top listings in Google, there's a risk you could damage your website performance and make it difficult to rank at all.

Let me tell you a secret about bloggers...

Articles about the latest SEO updates, techniques or tips are often written by interns, assistants, or even ghostwriters. Their job is to write articles. The majority of blog posts about SEO are rarely written by experts or professionals with the day-to-day responsibility of growing website traffic and achieving top rankings in search engines.

Can you learn from someone who doesn't even know how to do it themselves?

You can't. This is why you have to take the advice spread by blog posts with a grain of salt.

Don't get me wrong. I love bloggers. There are bloggers out there who practice and blog about SEO, and do it well. But it has become increasingly difficult to sort the wheat from the chaff.

Fear not. This chapter will disperse common misconceptions about SEO, show you how to avoid falling into Google's bad books and reveal how to stay up-to-date with how Google ranks websites.

But first, to understand how Google works today, we must understand a little bit about Google's history.

Old-school methods that no longer work.

In the early days of Google – over 15 years ago – Google started a smarter search engine and a better experience for navigating the World Wide Web. Google delivered on this promise by delivering relevant search engine results.

Internet users discovered they could simply type what they were looking for into Google — and BINGO — users would find what they needed in the top results, instead of having to dig through hundreds of pages. Google's user base grew fast.

It didn't take long for smart and entrepreneurially minded webmasters to catch on to sneaky little hacks for ranking high in Google.

Webmasters discovered by cramming as many keywords into the page as possible, they could get their website ranking high for almost any word or phrase. It quickly spiraled into a competition of who could jam the most keywords into the page. The page with the most repeated keywords won, and rose swiftly to the top of the search results.

Naturally, more and more spammers caught on and Google's promise as the 'most relevant search engine' was challenged. Webmasters and spammers became more sophisticated and found tricky ways of repeating keywords on the page and then completely hiding them from human eyes.

All of a sudden, grandma looking for 'holidays in Florida' would be left with the nasty surprise of arriving at a website about Viagra Viagra Viagra!

How could Google keep its status as the most relevant search engine, if people kept on spamming the results with gazillions of spammy pages, burying the relevant results to the bottom?

Enter the first Google update. Google released a widespread update in November 2003 codenamed 'Florida', effectively stopping spammers in their tracks. This update leveled the playing field by rendering keyword stuffing completely useless and restored balance to the force in the process.

And so began the long history of Google updates — making it harder for spammers to game the system and making ranking high a little more complicated for everyone.

Recent Google updates and how to survive them.

Fast-forward 15 years and ranking in Google has become extremely competitive and considerably more complex.

Simply put, everybody wants to be in Google. Google is fighting to keep its search engine relevant and must constantly evolve to keep on delivering relevant results to users.

This hasn't been without its challenges. Just like keyword stuffing, webmasters clued on to another way of gaming the system by having the most 'anchor text' pointing to the page.

If you are not familiar with this term, anchor text is the text contained in external links pointing to a page.

This created another loophole exploited by spammers. In many cases, well meaning marketers and business owners used this tactic to achieve high rankings in the search results.

Along came a new Google update. This time called 'Penguin' in 2012. Google's Penguin update punished websites with suspicious amounts of links with exact-matched anchor text pointing to a page.

Google discovered websites with hundreds of links with just one phrase likely didn't acquire those links naturally. This was a solid indicator the website owner could be gaming the system.

~

Shortly before this update, one year to be exact, many sites were ranking extremely high in Google by simply having a ridiculous amount of pages filled with crappy content.

Website owners discovered they could use Google to their advantage by spamming the Internet and uploading hundreds of pages on their websites, pretending to be a large authority or a large resource on their market.

Websites started flooding the search engine results with thousands of crappy articles generated by software. These articles were clearly created with the sole intention of gaming the system.

And so begins a familiar story. Google released an update called the Panda update, penalizing websites with dozens of duplicated articles and low quality content from ranking extremely high in search engines.

If you find these changes alarming, don't. How to recover from these changes, or to prevent being penalized by these updates, is covered in later chapters.

In this short history of Google's game changing updates, there lies a powerful lesson in how to achieve top rankings in Google and stay there.

The lesson is this....

If you want to stay at the top of Google, never rely on one tactic.

Always ensure your search engine strategies rely on SEO best practices.

How Google ranks websites.

Google has evolved considerably from its humble origins in 1993.

Eric Schmidt, once CEO of Google, once reported that Google considers over 200 factors to determine which sites rank higher in the results.

Today, Google assesses how many links are pointing to your website, how trustworthy these linking sites are, how many social mentions your brand has, how relevant your page is, how old your website is, how fast your website loads... the list goes on.

Does this mean it's impossible or hard to get top rankings in Google?

Nope. In fact, you have the advantage.

Very few business owners, marketers or even web designers know how to do SEO well. You simply have to know more than your competitors and act on this knowledge. The secret is to have a solid understanding of the factors Google uses to rank websites.

You might be wondering how you can find out the different factors that Google use?

Fortunately, there are a small handful of industry leaders who have figured it out and regularly publish their findings on the net, so you can get a working knowledge of what factors Google use to rank websites.

These surveys are typically updated every year, but don't be disheartened. The factors outlined in the surveys below are still massively accurate on how Google delivers search engine results today.

A short list of the strongest ranking factors:

-       Relevant terms/keywords

- Google +1
- Number of Backlinks
- Facebook shares
- Facebook total activity
- Facebook comments
- Pinterest activity
- SEO Strength of Backlinking URL/Page
- Facebook Likes
- Tweets

The above factors are from the Search Metrics Google Ranking Factors study. The Search Metrics study is fantastic for an in-depth look at the highest performing factors for ranking in Google. You can browse the full report by visiting the link below.

Search Metrics: Google Ranking Factors US
http://www.searchmetrics.com/en/knowledge-base/ranking-factors/

Another well known authority on the SEO industry, called MOZ (previously SEOMOZ), release a survey every two years, combining survey data from world leading SEOs, and a very detailed analysis of how Google functions today. MOZ then publish this information for free on their website.

MOZ Ranking Factors Survey
http://moz.com/search-ranking-factors

The Moz Ranking Survey was released for 2013, and is conducted every two years. But don't sweat it—they are still highly relevant, and I cover the 2014 algorithm updates in later chapters.

Take into account the above factors to determine how you optimize your website. If your competitors are ticking more of the above factors than your website, then it's very likely they are going to rank higher.

If your pages have more of the above factors than your competitors, then it is very likely you will beat them.

Combine this with an understanding of the recent updates to Google covered in later sections, and you will know what it takes to achieve top rankings in Google.

How to stay up-to-date with Google Updates

To hone your SEO chops, and make sure your website doesn't fall into Google's bad books, it's important for you to stay up-to-date with the Google Updates as they are released.

Fortunately, almost every time a major update is released, those updates are reported on by the entire SEO community and often publicly discussed and confirmed by Google staff.

A long, extended history of Google's Updates would fill this entire book, but with the resources below, you can always stay abreast of the new Google updates as they are rolled out. This is essential knowledge for anyone practicing SEO, at a beginner or an advanced level.

Matt Cutts Twitter Feed
https://twitter.com/mattcutts

Matt Cutts is the head of the Google webspam team, so by following Matt Cutts, you can regularly hear about the Google Updates direct from the source. Matt often announces Google Updates through his Twitter feed, which is a must-read for all budding SEO professionals.

Google Updates by Search Engine Round Table
http://www.seroundtable.com/category/google-updates

Search Engine Round Table is one of the industry's leading blogs on SEO. At the page above, you can browse all of the latest articles on the Google Updates as they are published by this leading authority.

Webmaster Central Blog
http://googlewebmastercentral.blogspot.com/

The Webmaster Central Blog by Google commonly discusses new updates as they are released. They also provide recommendations for SEO best practices to be used by webmasters.

Keyword research. The most important step of SEO.

Why is keyword research so important?

Keyword research is the first and most important stage of every SEO project.

Keyword research is the most important stage for two main reasons:

1. If you rank your website highly for the wrong keywords, you can end up spending lots of time and effort, only to discover that the keyword you have targeted doesn't receive any traffic.

2. If you haven't investigated the competitiveness of your keywords, you can end up investing lots of time and effort into a particular keyword, only to find it is far too competitive to rank, even on the first page.

These two pitfalls can be the ultimate decider on how successful any SEO project is.

This chapter will cover how to avoid these pitfalls and how to find the best keywords. First, we must define what a keyword is.

What exactly is a keyword?

If you are an SEO newbie, you may be wondering — what is a keyword?

Simply put, a keyword is any phrase you would like to appear for in Google's search results. A keyword can be a single word, or a keyword can also be a combination of words. If you are trying to target a single word, lookout! You will have your work cut out for you. Single word keywords are very competitive, and difficult to rank high for in the search results.

Don't be fooled or overwhelmed by the terminology. In some ways, 'keyword' is unnecessary jargon used by industry experts to sound professional, when it is just another word for a word.

If, on the other hand, you love industry jargon, here are some commonly used terms to describe different kinds of keywords:

Head-term: keywords with one to two words, i.e. classic movies.

Long-tail: keywords with three or more phrases, i.e. classic movies with subtitles

Keyword with intent: keywords that are obviously entered into Google by customers wanting to complete a certain action, i.e. 'buy jackets online'.

How to generate a massive list of keywords

There are many ways to skin a cat, and the same is true for finding the right keywords.

Before you can find keywords that receive loads of traffic in Google, you must first develop a list of potential keywords that are relevant to your business.

Relevance is vital.

If you spend your time trying to cast too wide a net, you can end up targeting keywords irrelevant to your target customers.

For example, if you are selling football jackets in an online store in the United States, examples of relevant keywords might be:

Buy football jackets
Buy football jackets online
Online football jackets store USA

Irrelevant keywords might be:

Football jacket photos
How to make your own football jacket
Football jacket manufacturers
How to design a football jacket

You can see how the first pool of keywords are much more relevant to the target audience of a seller of football jackets, and the second pool of keywords are related but unlikely to lead to customers.

Keeping relevance in mind, you must develop a list of potential keyword combinations to use as a resource, so you can then go and uncover the best keywords that receive a considerable amount of traffic each month in Google.

Listed below are powerful strategies you can use to help with generating this list.

1. Steal keywords from competitors.

If you're feeling sneaky, you can easily let your competitors do the heavy lifting for you and snatch up keywords from their websites.

There are many tools out there created for this sole purpose, but a simple tool, great for beginners and advanced SEO pundits, is the SEOBook keyword analyzer. If you enter a competitor's website into the tool at the below link, within seconds it will generate a pretty list of the most important keywords your competitor is using on the page. You can then use this keyword list for your research.

SEOBook Keyword Analyzer
http://tools.seobook.com/general/keyword-density/

2. Brainstorm your own master list.

Assuming competitors have been thorough with their research isn't always the best strategy. By brainstorming combinations of keywords, you can generate a giant list of potential keywords.

To do this, you simply need to sketch out a grid of words your target customer might use. Sketching out these ideas on paper or spreadsheet often works best to generate as many combinations as possible. Then you can combine these words and create a healthy-sized list of potential keywords.

Prefix
- buy
- where do I buy

Middle word
- NFL jerseys
- NFL uniforms
- NFL jackets

Suffixes
- online

Combined keywords
- NFL jerseys
- NFL jerseys online
- NFL uniforms
- NFL uniforms online
- NFL jackets
- NFL jackets online
- buy NFL jerseys

- buy NFL jerseys online
- buy NFL uniforms
- buy NFL uniforms online
- buy NFL jackets
- buy NFL jackets online
- where do I buy NFL jerseys
- where do I buy NFL jerseys online
- where do I buy NFL uniforms
- where do I buy NFL uniforms online
- where do I buy NFL jackets
- where do I buy NFL jackets online
- NFL jerseys
- NFL jerseys online
- NFL uniforms
- NFL uniforms online
- NFL jackets
- NFL jackets online

How to find keywords that will send traffic to your website

Now that you have a list of keywords, you need to understand how much traffic these keywords receive in Google. Without search traffic data, you could end up targeting keywords that receive zero searches. Armed with the right knowledge, you can target keywords that can lead to hundreds or even thousands of potential visitors every month.

First you have to sign up for a free Google Adwords account, link is provided below. Once signed in, you need to access the Keyword Planner tool.

To do this, sign in, click on 'Tools' in the top-menu, click on 'Keyword Planner', then click on 'Get search volume for a list of keywords or group them into ad groups', copy and paste your keywords into the box and click on 'Get Search Volume'.

Now click on 'Keyword Ideas' in the middle of the screen and viola!

Google Adwords
http://www.google.com.au/intl/en/adwords/

When you are finished, you will have the exact amount of times each keyword was searched for in Google.

Mmm. Fresh data. This is just the kind of data we need.

Now we know which keywords receive more searches than others, and more importantly, we know which keywords receive no searches at all. You can focus on keywords that will lead to more traffic to your website.

Ad group Ideas	Keyword Ideas					Download	Add all (4)
Keyword (by relevance)		Avg. monthly searches [?]	Competition [?]	Suggested bid [?]	Ad impr. share [?]	Add to plan
football jerseys		720	High	A$1.50	0%	»
football jerseys online		320	High	A$1.13	0%	»
football jackets		30	Medium	-	0%	»
where to buy football jerseys		10	Medium	A$2.12	0%	»

How to find keywords you can target for easy rankings

Now you need to find out how competitive your desired keywords are. Armed with an understanding of how competitive your desired keywords are, you can discover keywords that your website can realistically rank high for in Google.

Let's say you are a second-hand bookseller and you are going up against Amazon for 'book store online'. It's unlikely you are going to beat Amazon, Barnes and Noble and Borders.

But, maybe there's a gem hiding in your list that very few people are targeting, or have even thought of targeting — maybe something like 'antique book stores online'.

Remember, you have the advantage, if your competitors haven't thought of targeting your keyword, you simply have to do better SEO than they are doing and you have a really good chance at beating their rankings.

You need a way to wash this list and separate the ridiculously competitive keywords from the easy keywords no one has thought of.

There are many schools of thought on the best ways to do this. The most popular competitive research practices are listed below, with my thoughts on each.

1. Manually going through the list, looking at the rankings, and checking if low quality pages are appearing in the top results.

This is a good strategy, and you should always do this for your keywords. However, it is unreliable and you should always supplement it with real data.

2. Looking at how many search engine results are coming up in Google for your keyword.

The amount of results are listed just below the search box after you type in your keyword. This tactic is very common in online courses teaching SEO, but it is completely unreliable for determining if your site has a chance for ranking for this keyword. This is my least favorite strategy.

The reason? There may be a very low amount of competing pages for a particular keyword, but the sites ranked at the top of the results could be unbeatable.

3. Using the competition score from the Google Adwords Keyword Research tool.

Don't be tempted. This is a common tool, lauded on the Internet as an easy way to judge SEO competitiveness for keywords, and it just simply doesn't work!

The competition score included in the Google Adwords Keyword Research tool is intended for Adwords only. It is an indication of how many advertisers are competing for that particular keyword through paid advertising. It is completely irrelevant for SEO.

4. Using a competitive analysis tool, such as Market Samurai.

To get a realistic idea of your chances of ranking high for a particular keyword, you need to understand how strong the pages are that rank in the top-10.

A great tool for this is called Market Samurai.

With Market Samurai, you can simply enter in your keyword into their tool, click on 'competitiveness' and Market Samurai will show you the vital stats for the pages appearing in the top-10.

Using Market Samurai, you can compare the stats for the websites that are currently ranking to the stats for your own website. This gives an indication of how difficult it will be to rank for this keyword.

Market Samurai even makes it easy for you by color-coding the stats for each search result. The more boxes in red means the more difficult it will be to beat these rankings. The more boxes in green means the more opportunity you have to optimize these aspects of your page and beat the ranking.

Armed with this data, you can make an informed decision to reveal the keywords worth your time and effort.

Market Samurai
http://www.marketsamurai.com/

On-page SEO. How to let Google know what your page is about.

On-page SEO is the process of ensuring your website is readable to the search engines. Learning correct on-page SEO is not only an important step in ensuring Google picks up the keywords you want, it is an opportunity to achieve easy wins and improve the overall SEO of your website. This opens the door for better results across the board.

On-page SEO includes the following considerations:

1. Making sure website content is visible to search engines.
2. Making sure your website is not blocking search engines
3. Making sure search engines picks up the keywords you want them to.

Most on-page SEO you can do yourself, if you have a basic level of experience dealing with websites.

Please note, if you are not technically inclined: There are sections of this chapter that are quite technical. You should read these areas so you understand what has to be done to your website to achieve rankings in Google, but you can easily hire a web designer or web developer to implement the SEO techniques in this chapter, after you know what it takes to achieve top rankings.

How to structure your site for easy and automatic SEO

The best practices below will ensure your website is structured for better recognition by Google and other search engines.

1. Search engine friendly URLs.

Have you ever visited a web page and the URL looked like something like this?

http://www.examplesite.com/~articlepage21/post-entry321.asp?q=3

What a mess!

These kinds of URLs are a quick way to confuse search engines and website visitors. Clean URLs are much more logical, user friendly, and search engine friendly.

Below is an example of a clean URL:

http://www.examplesite.com/football-jerseys

Much better.

Take a quick look at Google's search engine results. You will see a very large portion of web sites in the top-10 have clean and readable URLs like the above example. And by a very large portion... I mean the vast majority.

Most website content management systems have search engine friendly URLs built into the website. It often is simply a matter of enabling the option in your website settings.

If your site doesn't have search engine friendly URLs, it's time for a 'friendly' chat with your web developer to fix this up.

2. Internal navigation

There are no limits on how to structure the navigation of your site. This can be a blessing or a curse.

Some people force visitors to watch an animation or intro before they can even access the website. In the process, some sites actually make it harder for visitors and more confusing for search engines to pick up the content on the site.

Other sites keep it simple by having a navigation bar running along the top of the site or running down the left-hand side of the browser window. This has pretty much become an industry standard for optimizing most websites.

By following this standard, you make it significantly easier for visitors and search engines to understand your site. If you intend to break this convention, you must understand it is very likely you will make it harder for search engines to pick up all of the pages on your site.

As a general rule, making it easier for users makes it easier for Google.

Above all else, your web site navigation must be made of real text links — not images!

If your main website navigation is currently made up of images, slap your web designer and change them now! If you do not have the main navigation featured in text, your internal pages will almost be invisible to Google and other search engines.

For an additional SEO boost, include links to pages that you want visible to search engines and visitors on the home page.

By placing links specifically on the home page, Google's search engine spider can come along to your web site and quickly understand which pages on your site are important and worth including in the search results.

How to make Google pick up the keywords you want

There are many misconceptions being circulated around the Internet about what to do, and what not to do, when it comes to optimizing keywords into your page.

Some bloggers are going so far as to telling their readers not to put their keywords in the content of targeted pages at all. These bloggers — I'm not saying names — do have the best intentions and have really taken worry about Google's spam detection to the next level.

But it is complete madness.

Not having keywords on your page at all makes it almost impossible for Google to match your page with the keyword you want to rank for. If Google completely devalued having keywords on the page, Google would be a crappy search engine.

Think about it. If you search for 'Ford Mustang 65 Auto Parts' and arrive on pages without those words on the page at all, it's extremely unlikely you have found what you're looking for.

Google must be able to pick up the keywords on your page, and these keywords must be visible to your users.

The easy approach is to either create content around your keyword, or naturally weave your keyword into the page.

No, I'm not saying your page should look like the following...

'Welcome to the NFL jersey store. Here we have NFL jersey galore, with a wide range of NFL jerseys including women's NFL jerseys, men's NFL jerseys and children's NFL jerseys and much much more.'

This approach may have worked 10 years ago, but not now. Above all else, the keyword should appear naturally in your page. Any attempts to go well and truly crazy with your keywords is will not only look horrible, it may set off spam filters in search engines. Using your keyword naturally throughout the content and having it repeated a couple of times is more than enough.

It's really that simple.

How to get more people clicking on your rankings in Google

Meta tags have been widely misunderstood as the mysterious pieces of code on websites SEO professionals' mess around with, and the secret to attaining top rankings. This couldn't be further from the truth.

The function of the Meta tags is really quite simple. The Meta tags are bits of code on your website that control how your site appears in Google.

If you don't fill out your Meta tags, Google will automatically take text out of your site to create a listing. This is exactly what you don't want Google to do, otherwise it can end up looking like gibberish! By filling out these tags correctly, you can increase the number of people that click through to your site from the search engine results.

Below is an example of the Meta tag code.

<title>Paul's NFL Jerseys</title>

```
<meta description='Buy NFL jerseys online. Wide range of
colors and sizes.' />
```

Below is an example of how a page with the above Meta
tag should appear as a search engine result in Google:

Paul's NFL Jerseys
Buy Paul's NFL jerseys online. Wide range of colors and
sizes.
http://www.yoursite.com/

Pretty simple, huh?

The Title tag has a character limit of roughly 70 characters
in Google. Use anymore than 70 characters and it is likely
Google will truncate your Title tag in the search engine
results.

The Meta description tag has a character limit of roughly
155 characters. Just like the title tag, Google will shorten
your listing if it has any more than 155 characters in the
tag.

To change these tags on your web site you have three
options:

1. Use the software your website is built on. Most content
management systems have the option to change these tags.
If it doesn't, you may need to install a plugin to change
these tags.

2. Speak with your web designer or web developer to
manually change your Meta tags for you.

3. If you are a tech-savvy person and are familiar with HTML, you can change these tags in the code yourself.

Website load speed — Google magic dust

How fast (or slow) your website loads is another factor Google takes into account when deciding how high it should rank your pages in the search results.

A very well known Google ambassador, Matt Cutts, has even publicly admitted fast load speed is a positive ranking factor.

If your website is as slow as a dead snail, then it is very likely your website is not living up to its full potential in the search engines. If your website load time is average, improving the load speed is an opportunity for an easy SEO boost.

Not only is load speed a contributing factor to achieve top rankings in Google, extensive industry reports have shown for each second shaved off a website, there is an average increase of 7% to the website conversion rate. The faster your website loads, the more chance you have of people completing a sale or filling out an inquiry form. Clearly, this is not an aspect of your website to be overlooked.

Fortunately, there are a small handful of tools designed to make it easy to improve your load speed.

1. Google Page Speed Insights.

https://developers.google.com/speed/pagespeed/insights

With Google's great free tool, Page Speed Insights, you can enter your web address and Google will give you a score out of 100. You can see how well your load speed compares to other websites. Scores closer to 100 are near perfect.

After running a test on your website, the tool will give you a list of high priority, medium priority, and low priority areas for improvement. You can forward these on to your developer to speed up your site, or if you are a bit of a tech-head, you can have a crack at fixing these up yourself.

2. Pingdom Tools
http://tools.pingdom.com/

Pingdom Tools is a great tool for an overview of how long your site takes to load in different areas of the world, and also for a visual breakdown of the files on your site that are total resource hogs and slowing it down.

After the test is completed, if you scroll down you will see a list of the files each visitor's web browser has to download each time they visit your website. If you discover files that can be decreased in size, you can improve your website load speed.

Easy targets for improvements are large images. If you have any images over 200kb, these can usually be optimized and shrunk down to a fraction of the size without any loss in quality. Take a note of these files, send them to your web developer or web designer, and ask them to compress the files to a smaller file size.

The usual suspects — sitemaps.xml and robots.txt

Sitemaps.xml

Search engines automatically look for a special file on each website called the sitemaps.xml file. Having this file on your site is a must-have for making it easier for search engines to discover pages on your site.

This file is essentially a giant map to all of the pages on your site.

Fortunately, creating this file and getting it on to your site is a straightforward process.

Visit the website below. All you have to do is enter your web address and it will automatically create a sitemaps.xml file for you.

XML Sitemaps Generator
http://www.xml-sitemaps.com/

All you have to do now is ask your web developer or web designer to upload it into the main directory of your site, or do it yourself if you have FTP access. Once uploaded, the file should be publicly accessible with a web address like the below example:

http://www.yourwebsite.com/sitemaps.xml

Once you have done this, you should submit your sitemap to the Google Webmaster Tools account for your website.

If you do not have a Google Webmaster Tools account, the below article by Google gives simple instructions for web developers or web designers to set this up.

http://support.google.com/webmasters/bin/answer.py?hl=en&answer=34592

Login to your account and click on your website. Under 'site configuration' click 'sitemaps', and in the textbox, enter the full address to your website.

Robots.txt

Another must have for every website is a robots.txt file. This is another file that should sit in the same place as your sitemaps.xml file. The address to this file should look the same as the example below:

http://www.yoursite.com/robots.txt

The robots.txt file is a simple file that exists so you can tell the areas of your site you do *not* want Google to list in the search engine results.

There is no real boost from having a robots.txt file on your website, but it is essential you check it to ensure you don't already have one blocking areas of your site that you *do* want search engines to find.

The robots.txt file is just a plain text document, with contents that should look something like below:

```
# robots.txt good example

User-agent: *
Disallow: /admin
User-agent: *
Disallow: /logs
```

If you want your website to tell search engines to not crawl your website, it should look like the next example. If you *do not* want your entire site blocked, you must make sure it does *not* look like the example below. It is always a good idea to double check it is not set up this way, just to be safe.

```
# robots.txt - blocking the entire website

User-agent: *
Disallow: /
```

The forward slash in the above example tells the search engine's crawling software that everything on your site should not be visited. You should always check to make sure you do not already have a robots.txt file with the above code.

To create your robots.txt file, simply create a plain text document with Notepad if you are on Windows, or Textedit if you are on Mac OS. Make sure the file is saved as a plain text document, and use the 'robots.txt good example' as an indication on how it should look. Take care to list any directories you do not want search engines to visit, such as internal folders for staff, admin areas, CMS back-end areas, and so on).

If you don't think there are any areas you would like to block, you can skip your robots.txt file altogether, but just double check you don't have one that is blocking the whole site like the above example.

Duplicate content — canonical tags and other fun.

In the first chapter, I mentioned how Google Panda penalized websites with duplicate content. Unfortunately, many site content management systems will sometimes have multiple versions of one page.

For example, let's say your website has a product page on socket wrenches, but because of the system your website is built on, the exact same page can be accessed from multiple URLs from different areas of your website:

http://www.yoursite.com/products.aspx?=23213

http://www.yoursite.com/socket-wrenches
http://www.yoursite.com/tool-kits/socket-wrenches

In the search engine's eyes, this is confusing as hell and these multiple versions of the page are considered duplicate content.

To account for this, you should always ensure a special tag is placed on every page in your website, called the 'rel canonical' tag.

The rel canonical tag indicates the original version of a web page to search engines. By telling Google the page you consider to be the 'true' version of the page into the tag, you can indicate which page you want listed in the search results. You should typically choose the URL that will make the most sense to users and provide the best SEO benefit, which will generally be the URL that reads like plain English.

Using the earlier socket wrenches example, with the tag below, Google would be more likely to display the best version of the page in the search engine results.

```
<link rel="canonical
" href="http://www.yoursite.com/socket-wrenches
"/>
```

As a general rule, make sure you include this tag on every page on your site, shortly before the </head> tag in the code.

Link building. How to rank extremely high on Google

Why is link building so important?

The previous chapter described how to make your site visible to search engines and how to optimize keywords by using on page SEO. If you want to see your rankings move up by leaps and bounds, your site needs links.

You may have wondered what makes link building so important, especially when there are so many factors Google use to rank websites.

The truth is, links are such a strong factor that it is unlikely you will rank highly for a keyword if you are competing against quality websites with more links pointing to their pages.

When you think about it, links are the currency of the web. Each time a page links to another, it is a vote for the value of the page being linked to. If a page provides massive value to Internet users, it stands to reason it will be linked to from other sites. This is why links are such a strong factor in Google's algorithm.

Link building is the key to ranking your website high in the search engine results.

The dirty little secret no one wants to tell you about link building.

There are a lot of opinions circulating the Internet about the best kind of links to build to your site. So much so, they often escalate into heated discussions.

What is the best link? A link from a government site or from a high trafficked blog? Is it better to get a link from a highly relevant site or from a site with a lot of social media activity?

The dirty secret no-one wants to tell you about link building is *there is no single best kind of link.*

If this weren't the case, Google wouldn't work. Everyone would go out and find a way to spam their way to the top of the rankings very quickly. Having thousands of one type of link pointing to a page is suspicious and a clear sign that the site owner is gaming the system.

How to acquire links and what to avoid in link building

There are many stories floating around the Internet about business owners being slammed by Google for no good reason, but don't let the horror stories mislead you.

In most cases, what has really happened is the webmaster was doing something clearly suspicious, like building thousands of links to their website from link directories, and then their rankings suddenly dropped off from Google's top-10 search results.

If you don't exhibit overly spammy behavior in your link building, as a general rule you will be okay.

Following the best practices will ensure you acquire links correctly and don't break Google's terms of service:

1. Acquire links naturally and evenly over time. Your links should be attained consistently and organically. Don't go out and buy one thousand links pointing to your website in one week.

3. As a rule, don't purchase links. Buying links with the intention of boosting your rankings is against Google's terms of service and you risk being penalized. These kinds of links may work, but are generally not worth the potential damage, unless you are confident you know what you are doing.

5. Forget about link swapping or link trading schemes. These are completely obvious to Google, and either no longer work or may even may harm your site. This goes against common knowledge, but I've achieved countless number one rankings for ridiculously competitive keywords without ever swapping links. Link swapping is extremely time-consuming and completely unnecessary. You can get by without it.

6. Don't spam message boards or article sites with crappy content. This might work temporarily, but strategies like these are typically outdated in a very short time-frame.

7. There are paid networks out there that offer to build new links to your website for a low monthly fee each month. Never use them. These networks are against Google's terms of service and using them is a quick way to ensure you find yourself in hot water with Google.

Anchor text. What's all the fuss?

There has been a lot of controversy surrounding anchor text, as touched on in a previous chapter. Anchor text *was* one of the strongest factors for achieving top rankings.

If you are wondering what anchor text is, anchor text is the text contained in a link.

If you had one thousand links to your website with 'NFL football jerseys' as the link text and competing sites only had a handful of links with the same anchor text, it was very likely you would rank number one.

Enter Google Penguin, which effectively put an end for SEOs using 'exact match' anchor text as their strategy. It is just simply too risky. This was such a strong factor, many professional SEOs are still using this strategy to their own detriment.

Not only is it no longer as effective as it once was, building hundreds of 'exact match' links to a web site actually can prevent it from ranking for that keyword.

So then, you might wonder, what is the best way to build up anchor text?

It should be natural.

It is okay to have your targeted keyword in your anchor text, but it should not be the only keyword or the main keyword in all of your links, and there should be a mix of related keywords.

If you think about it, this is a pattern that all legitimate websites naturally attract. It defies logic that a quality website would automatically be referred to and linked with the exact same text throughout the entire World Wide Web.

Look over the below examples to see a bad anchor text profile compared to a natural anchor text profile:

Bad anchor text – external links
http://www.examplefootballbrand.com/football-jerseys.html
NFL football jerseys - 200 links

Good anchor text
http://www.examplefootballbrand.com/football-jerseys.html
examplefootballbrand – 50 links
NFL football jersey store - 10 links
NFL football jerseys- 5 links
http://www.example.com - 25 links

football jersey store - 5 links
football jerseys online - 5 links
football jacket store - 15 links
click here - 7 links

The above good anchor text example illustrates the natural way websites accumulate links over time. Your targeted keyword should not be the most linked phrase to the page.

You can learn a lot by looking at the search engine results ranking in Google, enter high ranking sites into Open Site Explorer, and looking at their anchor text. You'll notice almost every top ranking has natural anchor text, like the good example.

Track your link building efforts and keep it in a spreadsheet. This way you can monitor your anchor text and make sure it fits in with best practices.

Powerful link building strategies.

The link building strategies below will help you build up an asset of quality links pointing to your site, and give Google a helpful nudge to rank your site higher.

Guest posting

Guest posting is a fantastic way to generate high quality links to your website that Google will love. It's also a great strategy for generating referral traffic from other relevant websites. You can really hit two birds with one stone with guest posting, making it a great strategy.

To be successful in guest posting, you must really focus on creating quality content. As you are reaching out to other web site owners, you significantly increase your chances of them accepting your offer by providing great content.

You'll be surprised at the response you can get. Many blog owners welcome guest posts because it saves them time and money!

There is another strategy for using guest blogging to build links that many business owners and even SEOs aren't aware of. By reversing the strategy — in other words, by accepting guest posts on your website — you can often attract a great amount of links to your website.

Guest authors will usually go and tweet their articles to all of their friends, link to it from their website and so on. It's only natural that authors want as many people as possible to read their content.

So, if you want to double the potential amount links you can get, why not try both guest posting as well as accepting guest posts?

The tools below will help you get in front of guest posting opportunities, whether it's posting on other people's websites, or having authors post on yours.

My Blog Guest. Free to start. Packages start from $30 for pro-users.
http://myblogguest.com/

My Blog Guest puts you in touch with high quality bloggers. You can have bloggers contact you to post on your site, and you can also get in touch with bloggers with high-quality blogs to post on their website.

Postrunner. Starts at $10 per month.
http://postrunner.com

This tool does not offer a free option, but it is fantastic if you are using Wordpress on your website. By simply installing the Postrunner plugin you can have guest bloggers contribute to your blog, and approve the articles directly from the Wordpress back-end. This tool is just simply amazing and saves loads of time.

Link bait

Link bait is a new and effective strategy for building high-quality and powerful links on a large scale. Link bait is great because you create content once, but you can have thousands of people over the Internet literally sharing and linking to your content, while you sit back and put your feet up.

But what is link bait exactly? Link bait is any kind of massively compelling content that goes viral, and naturally acquires links from other websites as a result.

Sound cool? It is. But there is an art to creating link bait successfully.

You need to make your content free and shareable. Your content must be so valuable it would almost be worth paying for.

To create this content, you should use your expertise or even hire researchers to put together juicy industry content that lends itself to being shared.

Wrap up this content into a whitepaper, top-10 list, or an easy to understand infographic, or a printable resource and you have made it compelling for visitors to read and to share.

Once you have created your content, you have to promote your content to enough readers for it to kick off.

Promote this content heavily through your entire website and social media accounts. Prompt readers to share the post at the bottom of the content. Make sharing the content as easy as possible and you will maximize the results.

If you really want to take link baiting to the next level, write and publish a compelling press release about your link bait content. With a press release it can be exposed to thousands of journalists and potentially has a chance of attracting media coverage.

You might be wondering what a successful link baiting campaign looks like. I've listed some great examples below.

The Facebook Marketing Guide
http://blog.kissmetrics.com/facebook-marketing/

KissMetrics' long list of marketing guides on their website is a fantastic example of link bait.

I Can Haz Cheezburger
http://icanhas.cheezburger.com/
Cat videos have grown a bit tiresome over the Internet, but this massively viral website is a great example of link bait — the entire website is link bait.

101 Motivational Business Quotes
http://www.quicksprout.com/2009/12/07/101-motivational-business-quotes/
Excellent example of a great link bait article that went massively viral, but could be easily outsourced for pennies on the dollar.

Use the resources below to speed up your link bait creation and promotion.

Types of link bait

- Infographics
- How to guides.
- Beginner guides
- Breaking news
- Top 10 lists
- Industry reports

Pictochart.
http://piktochart.com/
Great service for infographic generation, has an easy drag and drop interface to put infographics together in minutes. Free package offers 10 themes.

Prlog.
http://www.prlog.org/
Prlog offers entry-level free press release syndication services, with additional coverage for an added fee.

PRNewswire.
http://www.prnewswire.com/
Many PR firms will simply write a press release and then release it to PRNewswire and charge a premium for doing so. Cut out the middleman, write up your press release yourself and you can get massive PR for a fraction of the cost of hiring a PR agent. Packages start at $425 USD and scale up for increased syndication.

Article links

Submitting articles with content relevant to your industry is an easy opportunity to build up links to your site with the keywords you are targeting. The more articles you publish, the more links you will have pointing to your site.

To ensure your articles fit in with Google's rules and regulations, and don't set of spam triggers, your articles must be unique and create real value for visitors.

So focus on quality.

Should you submit the same article to multiple web sites? Nope. The additional links are unlikely to count. Google's software is pretty smart at picking up duplicate content.

Focus on creating multiple quality unique articles for a bigger result. Spread them out evenly between the different article directories and you will get the best outcome.

Ezinearticles
http://ezinearticles.com/

Go articles
http://goarticles.com/

Articles Base
http://www.articlesbase.com/

Amazines
http://www.amazines.com/

EHow
http://www.ehow.com/

Hubpages
http://hubpages.com/

Broken link building/link outreach

Broken link building is a new, but powerfully effective strategy. With this new strategy, you can reach out to quality sites with broken outgoing links on their pages, and use this as an opportunity to convince the site administrator to update those broken links with a link to your site.

Use the below resources to search for related websites with broken links. When you find a broken link, let them know the broken link exists and you have an alternative resource on your site that will benefit their readers. You will get a greater response if you discover the original content on the page the broken link points to and create a similar page on your site. This makes it very easy for the webmaster to point the link to your potential replacement page.

Use the formulas below to find potential pages with broken links, replacing 'keyword' with the keyword you are targeting:

keyword useful links
keyword useful resources
keyword useful sites
keyword useful websites
keyword recommended links
keyword recommended resources
keyword recommended sites
keyword recommended websites
keyword suggested links
keyword suggested resources
keyword suggested sites
keyword suggested websites
keyword more links
keyword more resources
keyword more sites
keyword more websites
keyword favorite links
keyword favorite resources
keyword favorite sites

keyword favorite websites
keyword related links
keyword related resources
keyword related sites
keyword related websites

If you want to automate this whole process, the tools below will do the heavy lifting for you, and give you a list of sites with broken links and contact details so you can reach out to the webmaster.

Broken link index. Free
http://brokenlinkindex.com/
Broken link index is not a complete database of broken link opportunities, but it will find some opportunities and will save precious time.

Broken linkbuilding. $67 monthly.
http://www.brokenlinkbuilding.com/
This tool is more comprehensive, but comes at a price. By simply typing in the keywords you are targeting, the broken linkbuilding tool will go through and find a sizable amount of broken link opportunities. Saves time and finds quality opportunities.

Broken Brand Mentions

Use the below tools to track mentions of your brand. If you see a mention of your brand without a link back to your site, send a quick email to the author, and they will often be more than happy to link back to your site.

Brand monitoring sites:

Socialmention.com
Mention.com
Freshwebexplorer.moz.com
www.google.com/alerts

Directory links

Directory linking is a tried and true form of link building, but has received flack in recent years. This is due to Google devaluing spammers who build truckloads of directory links to their website. Directory links should not make up any more than 20% of your total links.

Despite the controversy, directory links do work, but they must be relevant and from quality websites, i.e. not sites with web addresses like seolinksdirectory.com or freelinksdirectory.com. Sites like these just smell of spam!

To find relevant directories, use the below search terms in Google, replacing 'keyword' with your targeted keyword or industry, and you will find a list of relevant websites:

keyword + submit
keyword + add url
keyword + add link
keyword + directory
keyword + resources

MOZ also publishes a list of 400+ reputable link directories, available for free trial and paid members http://www.moz.com/directories

Video link building

Google loves videos, and it especially loves videos from video juggernaut YouTube. If you want the opportunity to capture visitors from the world's largest video search engine, posting videos will considerably help your SEO.

Post relevant how-to guides, industry news updates, and instructional videos for the best response from users and the most views. Then make sure you link to the relevant pages on your website in the description.

The key to success in video link building is to ensure the video and your description are related. You should aim to have your targeted keyword or relevant keywords occurring on the page somewhere.

And don't worry. Your video doesn't have to be on par with the latest masterpiece by Martin Scorsese. It can be a simple, 5 or 10-minute video, educating visitors with useful knowledge about your topic.

Use the tools below to quickly create videos and upload them to the web.

EZVid
http://www.ezvid.com

EZVid is a fantastic, free tool for recording screencasts. You can start recording whatever is on your screen with a click of the mouse, and finish with a high-quality video ready to upload to video sites within minutes. Only for Windows users.

Screenr
http://www.screenr.com/

Screenr is a fantastic, free video recording web app that allows you to record high-quality screencasts from the convenience of your own web browser. You can download the video files in high quality after you have finished, and it works on both Windows and Mac computers.

Veoh
http://www.veoh.com/

Veoh provides easy video upload & submission.

YouTube
http://www.youtube.com/

YouTube is a must for video submissions, and has a very open policy to accepting all kinds of videos.

Metacafe
http://www.metacafe.com/

Another great video submission service, with an open policy for accepting all kinds of videos.

Stealing competitor's links.

Stealing competitor's links is an old-school tactic receiving a resurgence in popularity in recent times, due to Google's increased focus on quality links from quality sites.

If your competitor has done all the heavy lifting, why not take advantage of their hard work? Use the below sites to do an export of your competitor's backlinks, go through those links and see if there are any opportunities for you to get a link pointing to your own website.

Ahrefs Backlink Checker – Free to try, then $79 per month. http://www.ahrefs.com/

Majestic SEO Backlink Checker – Free to try, then £29 British pounds per month.

Paid links

While Google clearly states that any kind of 'paid' links are against their terms-of-service, these below link building tactics work well and fly under the radar.

Needless to say, if you're feeling daring, you've been warned and I take no responsibility for what happens as a result of the below strategies.

Paid reviews.

There are sites that will get you quickly in contact with bloggers with an established audience, who you can pay a small fee to review your product or service.

This is a dead-simple and extremely easy way to get a link to your site. Try sponsoredreviews.com, reviewme.com and payperpost.com

Donate to charities & non-profits.

Charities and non-profits sites often have a donors page. Search for "site:.org + donors" or "site:.org + sponsors" in Google for a list of organizations that have these pages, offer a donation, and request a listing on the page.

Better Business Bureau.

Links from the Better Business Bureau are among the best links you can receive. Better Business Bureau links will pass authority and trust. Check your listing to see if you are already linking back to your website, and if you're not already a member with a listing, then sign up!

Social media and SEO.

Is social media important for SEO?

Now that social media has become so commonplace, important content is not only linked to, it is shared, liked, tweeted, and pinned. How people use the Internet has drastically changed.

This begs the question.... Has Google adapted their ranking factors to take into account these new behaviors?

Many of the independent studies on Google's algorithm, mentioned earlier, show a large correlation with high-ranking pages typically having strong social media activity. But correlation doesn't necessarily mean causation.

In other words, there are many people in the SEO community who say we don't know for certain if social media activity is in fact a positive ranking signal in Google's search results... It could just be that the high value pages that have a tendency to rank high, also naturally attract a high amount of social activity.

I'm of the belief that 'a link is a link'. Every time you share a link on a social media site pointing back to your site it is a free and very easy link to build, increasing the overall chances of your website ranking high.

It also increases the possibility of your website getting more traffic and referral links from the subsequent social activity.

And I've found, as a rule, the sites I've worked on with strong social media followings typically tend to get higher rankings much faster...

So to keep things simple, I always use social media as part of my SEO strategies as a best practice — and recommend that you do the same.

By integrating social media into your SEO strategy, not only could you potentially get a SEO boost, it's a great way to re-engage your existing customer base, and get some cheap and free traffic!

Facebook and SEO

To improve your site's Facebook social activity, be sure to share content from your website on your own Facebook page on a regular basis.

Each time you do this, you receive more exposure from your fan base, and you also build up the social activity around the content on your website. Be careful to mix this up with relevant, engaging content from other sites for your user base, so you don't turn them off.

As a rule of thumb, for every one link you share about your brand on your Facebook page, share three pieces of content about topics your customer base would be interested in.

Using Twitter for SEO

Twitter is so prevalent with discussion on the world's latest events. In many cases, groundbreaking news stories are released on Twitter before the world's major news outlets.

You can use Twitter as part of your SEO strategy by creating a Twitter page and using a service like ifthen.com or hootsuite.com and to schedule your tweets.

Schedule tweets to your pages and start building up your tweet counts on your pages. Mix this up with relevant and informative tweets about your industry, otherwise, just like Facebook, you risk irritating your follows.

If you want to encourage website visitors to tweet your content for you, include a 'tweet this page' link on every page or blog post on your web site.

Tweetdeck. Free.
http://www.tweetdeck.com

Free and easy Twitter management software. You can install Tweetdeck on your computer and manage your whole Twitter account from inside the program. Popular features include managing multiple accounts, scheduling tweets, and arranging feeds so you only see updates from Twitterers you're interested in.

Hootsuite. Free to start. $10 monthly for power users. http://www.hootsuite.com

More advanced than Tweetdeck, you can use Hootsuite to schedule tweets, analyze social media traffic, manage multiple accounts, create social media reports to monitor your success and much more. Recommended for power users or automating multiple accounts.

Other social networks

Hey let's face it. We'd all love to play around on social networks all day, but we don't have an unlimited amount of time to be coming up with great ideas and sharing them on endless social media accounts.

If you have limited resources, focus on Facebook, Google Plus and Twitter.

If you are looking for an extra edge, or maybe you have an army of helpers waiting for your command, you can gain significant boosts by expanding your social activity to several social media websites.

Setup an account on the below networks, posting on the networks most relevant to your business.

Linkedin
http://www.linkedin.com

Linkedin is the Facebook for professionals. Linkedin is a fantastic networking tool to use if you are in the business-to-business industry and are looking to build up your personal brand or the brand of your site. If you want to increase your effectiveness on Linkedin, join groups and participate in discussions, post relevant updates about your industry and post your content in the feed.

Pinterest
http://www.pinterest.com

Pinterest has become one of the fastest growing social networks in a very short time frame. Pinterest's fast growing user base is primarily made up of women. The site has effectively turned into a giant shopping list of wish list items. If your target audience is women, you should be on Pinterest.

Google Plus
http://www.google.com/intl/en/+/business/

Google has been consistently rewarding businesses on their own social network. A lot of businesses still aren't using Google Plus, so this is an opportunity to get an advantage over competitors, especially with Google Plus being reported as being one of the strongest ranking factors.

Social media analytics

If you start investing time and effort building up your social media profiles, you will want to track your results so you can separate the parts of your strategy that are successful and not so successful.

Social media analytics is different compared to most other web analytics, because most social analytics are geared to measuring the conversation and interaction of your fan base with your brand. Using the software listed below, you can monitor results and get valuable insights on how to improve your social media efforts.

Viral Heat. Free for 14-days. $9 per month for regular use.
https://www.viralheat.com/

Viral Heat is a new player into the social media analytics field. You can monitor conversations about your brand on Facebook, Twitter, blogs and much more.

Sprout Social. Free for 30-days. $39 per month for regular use.
http://sproutsocial.com/features

Another great web analytics package that allows you to track the performance of your social media profiles over time. Sprout Social has the same essential core functionality than Viral Heat, but has a longer free trial and more suited to advanced level use.

Google Analytics Social Tracking. Free

https://support.google.com/analytics/answer/1683971?h
l=en

Google Analytics social tracking features are great for
tracking social interactions that occur when visitors are on
your website. It does require an experienced developer to
setup, but it is free and provides valuable insights on how
users behave when they visit your site.

Web analytics in a nutshell. How to measure your success.

Web analytics have made it much easier to calculate the return-on-investment of SEO and other marketing efforts down to the dollar.

Read on to gain a greater awareness of the inner workings of your marketing.

Why use Google Analytics?

You may have heard about Google Analytics, or otherwise known as Universal Analytics, by Google. Google Analytics is the web analytics tool currently used by the majority of websites. It does have its quirks, but it is the best all round analytics tool available to us for understanding website traffic. And it's free.

If you do not have Google Analytics installed, put down this book, install Google Analytics now and then slap your web developer. I'm not joking. Without Google Analytics set up, it's not unlike trying to pilot an airplane blindfolded. Without Google Analytics it's almost impossible to spot patterns or trends in traffic and identify issues so you can solve them before they turn into greater issues.

How to use Google Analytics

Let me tell you something you may find shocking. Most data on its own is useless. You heard correctly. For real awareness and actionable insights, we need to be able to compare data and identify trends over time.

There are two ways to analyze and understand data in Google Analytics.

1. Compare two date ranges. Click on the date field input in Google Analytics. Both date time frames must be equal, otherwise you will obscure your data. Useful date comparisons include comparing this week's performance to last week's performance, last month's performance to the month prior, and last month's performance to the same month the previous year.

2. Another way is to simply look at the charts over a long period of time and look for trends, and not compare date ranges. This approach provides visual confirmation of the general direction your traffic is heading, but you will be unable to compare specific percentages of moving trends.

Note: Seasonality is a factor affecting many websites. Often, you will have months performing worse than previous months, but this may not be an indicator you website is performing poorly. It could be that the market of your business experiences a downward trend in certain months of the year. To see if your website is experiencing a downward trend but still performing well, compare the current month's traffic to the same period the previous year. If you are seeing increases, then you know your website is still performing well.

Traffic Sources

Traffic sources are an area of Google Analytics you should be spending a lot of time in. Without keeping a close eye on your traffic sources it is almost impossible to make informed judgments about the performance of your site.

In the traffic sources section you can see the actual amounts of traffic you have received from a given source. The Google organic section is of special interest, as this is the non-paid traffic you are receiving from Google, and a large portion of this traffic comes as a result of your rankings in Google.

Organic traffic report

The Organic Traffic report is an essential report within Google Analytics for monitoring the performance of your site. Within the Organic Traffic report, you can actually see how many times you receive a visitor from search engines and what keyword they searched for. You can compare keyword performance to previous months, using the date comparison tool mentioned earlier, making it much easier to monitor performance over time.

Google has made some changes to Google Analytics that have many search engine marketers and marketing professionals up in arms. Early in 2012, Google changed this tool to hide some of the keyword information typed into browsers by logged in users. Thanks Google!

Each time someone types in a phrase into Google, if they are currently signed into any Google account while browsing, the keyword the visitor typed in will now show up as a 'not provided' keyword in Google Analytics. When this happens, you have no idea what that person typed into Google before arriving at your website.

The portion of these visitors has gradually increased, but don't be too concerned, we can still measure the overall performance of Google organic traffic by looking for total increases or decreases in amounts of organic visitors.

To view the Organic Traffic report within Google Analytics, click on the Traffic Sources tab on the left sidebar, click on Search, and then click on Organic.

Advanced segments

Imagine if you could narrow down any report to a particular segment of your audience, like paid traffic, search engine traffic, mobile traffic, iPad users, and so on. This feature exists and it is called Advanced Segments.

Advanced Segments are powerful because you can identify segments of your audience that may generate more inquiries or sales than other customers. You can even identify portions of your audience who are having trouble using your site.

To use Advanced Segments, you simply have to click on the 'Add Segment' tab at the top of every page within Google Analytics.

Common web analytics terms.

Pageviews

A pageview is counted each time a user loads a page on your site in their web browser.

Unique pageview

A unique pageview is similar to a pageview, but a unique pageview only counts a pageview once per visitor.

Session

A session is what occurs when a visitor arrives at the website, and then at some point closes the browser. If that visitor returns again, this is counted as an additional session.

User

If a user visits your website, and then returns at a later stage, this is counted as one unique user.

Bounce Rate

If a visitor visits your site, and then leaves without visiting any more pages, this is a bounce. The percentage of visitors who bounce is your bounce rate. A common question among markets and business owners is what is a good bounce rate? There is no general rule. Bounce rates vary greatly between websites and industries. If you find a particular page with a very high bounce rate (+70%), this could be an indicator the visitors do not find the content relevant.

Conversion rate

One of the most important metrics to monitor is your website conversion rate. A conversion rate is the ratio of visitors who complete a desired action. The action could be filling out an inquiry form, downloading a product, or buying something from you. If you receive one hundred visitors, and three of these visitors complete a sale, this would be a three percent conversion rate.

Goals

Goals are custom goals you can set up within Google Analytics to track the particular business goals you may have for your website.

Common goals to set up include newsletter signups, product downloads, inquiry form completions, and so on.

Other web analytics tools

There are many web analytics tools out there to help with improving the performance of your site. Google Analytics is great for understanding your traffic performance, but if you want to delve deeper, check out the following tools for greater insights.

Crazy Egg. Free to start, Starts at $9 month for premium features.
http://www.crazyegg.com

If you want a visual indication of how visitors behave on your website once they arrive, Crazy Egg is a fantastic tool. With Crazy Egg, you can get heat maps of where visitors click on the page. You can also see heat maps of how far visitors scroll down the page.

Optimizely. Free for 30-days, then starting at $17 monthly.
http://www.optimizely.com

Optimizely is an award-winning split-testing analytics tool. With Optimizely you can split test different variations of your website, and see which version makes more sales or conversions.

Troubleshooting common SEO problems & how to fix them.

Dealing with Google can be massively frustrating at times. Customer support barely exists, and trying to understand why your site isn't playing well with Google can spiral into a wild goose chase.

Don't let Google's lack of customer support or the horror stories dishearten you. Most of the time, if a site is experiencing Google problems, it is only temporary. SEO problems are rarely irrecoverable.

Usually it's a simply matter of finding out what the underlying cause of the problem is — more often than not, the cause isn't what the popular blog posts are saying it might be. This sometimes means fixing several items. Once all are fixed, you have stacked the deck in your favor and you are more likely to make a speedy recovery.

This chapter outlines common SEO problems that plague web site owners. For reference sake, I've outlined potential solutions and advice on where to go if you need more help.

If you are not at all technically inclined, I urge you to read the section on getting additional advice, or even considering getting professional help if your website is experiencing serious SEO issues.

What to do when your website is not listed in Google at all

This is a common problem among webmasters and business owners alike.

If you have just launched a brand new website, it is possible Google has not crawled your site yet. You can do a quick spot check by typing 'site:yourwebsiteaddress.com' into the Google search bar and checking to see if your website comes up at all. If it doesn't, it is likely Google's spider hasn't crawled your website, and effectively doesn't know it exists.

Typically, all that's required to pick up your site is to generate a handful of links of your site, and some social activity.

Tweeting a link to your website is a quick way to ensure your website is indexed by Google's software. Ask a friend with a fair sized social media following to post a link to your site as a favor, and you will see results a lot sooner. Try and share your website from a handful of social networks for faster results.

Check Google again in 24 hours with the 'site:www.yoursite...' search query and see if any pages from your site comes up. If you do see pages, this means Google has indexed your web site.

If this doesn't work, ask your web designer to setup Google Webmaster Tools for you, login, and see if there are any errors. If there are errors, Google will outline the steps to fix them, so Google can see your site.

What to do when your business is not ranking for your own business name

A business not coming up in the top position in Google for searches for the business name is a surprisingly common issue among brand new websites. Google is smart, but sometimes you need to give Google a nudge to associate your new site with the name of your brand.

This solution is typically easily fixed by building links to your site, with some of the links with your brand name as the anchor text. This can take anywhere up to a couple of weeks for Google to see these links, connect the dots and realize your site is the real deal.

The fast way to get the ball rolling is to do a quick search for the business directories used in your country — Whitepages, Yellow Pages, Yelp, and so on — fill out a listing for your business on each site and include a link back to your web site. The more links the better, but you should be aiming for a minimum of 50 links. In 95% of cases this will solve the problem of a site not coming up in the top results for searches for the business name.

If this doesn't work, setup Facebook and Twitter accounts for your business, filling out as much information about your business as possible in the profile. Then do a post a day for about two weeks, mixing in links to your website in the posts.

If you still can't get your web site ranking high enough, use Open Site Explorer to spy on competing sites ranking higher for the brand name. Do their pages have more backlinks than the total amount of links to your site? If this is the case, you are going to need to build more links.

What to do when your rankings have dropped off

Here's a sad truth about SEO. If you achieve a top ranking, it may not keep its position forever. There are billions of web pages competing for top positions in Google. New websites are being created every day. It requires an ongoing effort to keep pages ranking high.

If your rankings have dropped off from the top position and are slowly moving their way down the search results, it's likely your competitors have simply acquired more links or more social activity. Use Open Site Explorer to spy on competitors, find out how many backlinks they have, how much social media activity they have, and set these amounts as your target to build your rankings back up.

Next, it's time to start a link building campaign with the targeted keywords as outlined in the chapter on link building.

If you are worried you may have been penalized by the recent updates to Google, such as the Penguin update or the Panda update, read the next section for common recovery steps.

What to do when your website has been penalized by the Penguin update

The recent updates to Google have many website owners worried. The media circus are partly to blame for this, but the controversy surrounding the Panda and Penguin updates have created the misconception that most traffic issues are caused by these updates.

The real truth — these updates have affected a fraction of websites and these website owners are a very loud minority.

In most cases, if your rankings have dropped off, your competitors have simply acquired more 'SEO Juice' to their pages, and it's time to pick up your game. If your pages have moved down a few positions, refer to the above section on the steps to recovery.

If your rankings have completely disappeared from Google's top-30, and they were previously ranking in the top-10, then, it is possible you may have been penalized from Google's Penguin update. Follow the below steps to confirm if this was the case and follow the recommended steps to make a recovery.

Read on with caution. Penalties from the Panda and Penguin updates are difficult to diagnose and even more difficult to heal. If you are out of your depth, you may need to seek professional help to make a speedy recovery.

1. Check Google Webmaster Tools.

Any website owners that have had a *manual* penalty imposed on Google will receive a notice like the one below. Log in to your Google Webmaster Tools account to see if you have received a notice like the one below:

'Google Webmaster tools notice of detected unnatural links to....'

We've detected that some of your site's pages may be using techniques that are outside of Google's Webmaster Guidelines....'

If you have witnessed the above message in Google Webmaster tools, Google has placed a manual penalty on your website as a result of the new Google updates. If you do not see the above message, then it is unlikely you have received a manual penalty from Google.

2. Check your link profile.

Use Open Site Explorer, and Majestic SEO and look at the links pointing to the page you suspect may have been penalized. Do the same for the competing pages that are currently ranking in the top position for your keywords.

Look for the indicators below to confirm if your website has been penalized by the Google updates.

1. Your web site has a much larger quantity of links than competitors, but isn't ranking in the top-50 for the same keyword.

If you have a significantly larger amount of links pointing to your page than competing websites, and your site is nowhere to be seen in the top-50 (but it was before), then you may have been penalized by the Penguin update.

2. Your website has a very large quantity of links from shoddy looking web sites, e.g. sites that look like the following, seolinksdirectory.com, addurlsfree.com, freelinkdirectory.com and so on.

3. Your page has anchor text pointing to the page for your targeted keyword greater than 20% as a general rule. Example; if 90% of the links pointing to the page have a targeted keyword as the anchor text, it is possible you may have been penalized by the Penguin update.

4. Use the Panguin tool at www.panguintool.com to see if you have any sudden traffic declines around the times of the Google updates. If your traffic has not recovered, then it is possible your site has been penalized by Penguin.

Google Penguin recovery steps

The following list walks you through the process required to heal a website penalized by Google Penguin. Please note, before you do any of these items, you must be absolutely confident your site has been affected by these updates. If your website has not been penalized by these updates, the below steps could do more harm than good to your website.

If you are certain, it is highly recommended you seek professional advice.

1. Export all the backlinks to the page that has been penalized, using your Google Webmaster tools account, Open Site Explorer and Majestic SEO. Compile all of the links together into an Excel spreadsheet.

Go through and group together the links on spammy domains (e.g. freelinks.tv, seolinksdirectory.com, freeseolinks.com, bizlinks.biz and so on).

2. Go visit each of these spammy sites and look for a link removal page. If there is no link removal page, find a contact page and request the website administrator to remove your link from their website. Provide a link to the page in question in your message to make it easier for the webmaster.

If you cannot locate any contact information for the website, use Domain Whois (whois.com) to find the site owner's contact details and contact the owner directly.

Document all of these efforts in a spreadsheet with a date, time and outcome.

3. After you have allowed 1-2 weeks for the webmasters to remove the links to your site, find the spammy links for the websites you have not been able to remove and put each of these bad links into a plain text file, with each link placed on a new line.

Log into Google Webmaster Tools and submit these links using the 'Remove URLs' page in the 'Optimization' section. Again, if you are uncertain about what you are doing, consult a professional SEO otherwise you could risk doing more harm than good.

4. File a reconsideration request in Google Webmaster tools. This should only occur after you have made a very thorough effort to remove your links manually and then disavowed the links through the disavow link tool.

You must submit a request to Google to let them know you believe you have been blocked by the Penguin update, and have gone to great efforts to clean up the link spam.

To do this, visit the following URL after logging into your webmaster tools account:

File a reconsideration request
https://www.google.com/webmasters/tools/reconsideration?pli=1

5. Await response and monitor rankings changes.

As mentioned, recovering from a Google Penguin penalty is not something anybody should do without a base level of professional SEO experience and complete confidence the website has been penalized by the Penguin update.

These steps have been included for those with SEO experience, and to illustrate the steps required to recover from a Penguin penalty.

It is highly recommended you speak with an expert before doing any of the above steps to attempt to recover from a penalty.

How to seek professional help for free

Finding the right SEO help can be frustrating for website owners. There is a lot of information to navigate, with varying levels of quality and accuracy. It's hard to get in touch with SEO practitioners who are at the top of their field.

That said, there are sites that can put your questions in front of the world leading experts of almost any topic for free. Use the below websites for highly technical responses, and you can create an army of Internet experts to try to solve your problem for you.

The key to success with the below resources is to be specific. The more specific you are and the more information you provide increases your chances that you will receive a detailed answer that will point you in the right direction.

For greater results, post your question on *all* of the sites below and sit back and wait for the answers to come in. You will get more answers, and will be in a better position to consider which solution is best.

MOZ Q&A
http://moz.com/community/q

MOZ's Q&A forums used to be private, but have just recently released this feature open to the public. Here you can speak with a large number of SEO professionals directly and attract high quality answers to your questions. Great for SEO specific problems.

Pro Webmasters
http://webmasters.stackexchange.com/

The Pro Webmasters Q&A board can have your questions answered by webmasters of high performing websites.

Quora
http://www.quora.com

Quora is an all round Q&A posting board, where you can get a question answered on almost anything. On Quora, questions are often answered by high profile experts. Marketers, business owners, you name it, there are many leading industry authorities posting answers to questions on Quora.

Stack Overflow
http://stackoverflow.com/

Created by the founders of Pro Webmasters, Stack Overflow is a community of web site developers answering web development related questions. If you have a very technical question related to your site or if you just want to keep your web developer honest by getting a second opinion, Stack Overflow is a great resource for getting highly technical questions answered.

Wordpress Answers
http://wordpress.stackexchange.com/

If your site is built on Wordpress, it's inevitable you will eventually encounter some kind of technical hurdle. The Wordpress Answers Q&A board is a great resource to seek out help.

Indexing & SERP Display Problems and Questions
High Rankings Forum
http://www.highrankings.com/forum/index.php/forum/67-indexing-and-serp-display-problems-and-questions/

This discussion board on the High Rankings forum is specifically related to users having trouble getting their site to rank in Google. Here you will find answers for tough questions with a fast turnaround time. As is the case with all discussion boards, you can have a lively discussion about any topic, but you should always cross-reference and verify any information you receive.

Local SEO. SEO for local businesses.

Why use Local SEO?

Unless you have been living under a rock, you have seen the listings for local business appearing at the top of some search results in Google. The local listings — previously known as Google Place page listings, now known as Google+ pages — are a great tool for local businesses looking to get more customers.

Local search results differ from traditional 'organic' search results, as they are a search engine result representing a local business, instead of a web page like normal search results.

Users can see business contact details at a glance, and find the information they need, instead of having to click through and dig around a clunky business web site.

Local SEO can be a powerful tool to attract traffic. In many cases, local SEO can lead to many more inquiries for local businesses than regular SEO rankings.

Does this mean you should scrap traditional SEO in favor of local SEO? Nope. You can do both, and increase the amount of potential traffic your website can receive.

How to rank high with local SEO

Ranking high with local SEO takes a much different approach than traditional SEO. Google's algorithm is looking for a different set of signals to determine the popularity of a business and decide how high to rank it in the search results.

If you think about it, if a restaurant is really popular in a city, a whole bunch of links from websites all over the world probably isn't the best factor to determine how popular the business is in a local area.

A better indicator of the importance of a local business would be mentions of the business name and phone number, customer reviews, and how close the business is to the area being searched.

Below is a list of the most important ranking factors Google use for local listings.

Local search ranking factors

1. Physical address in City of search.
2. Proper category associations (you must choose the most accurate category for your business).
3. Proximity of business to the center of the city being searched.

4. Domain authority of web site (amount and quality of links pointing to web site).
5. Quantity of structured citations (amount of pages listing your business name and phone number).
6. City, State in Places Landing Page Title.
7. Quantity of Google Places reviews.
8. Quality of structured citations (quality of the websites listing your business name and phone number).
9. Local phone area code on place page.
10. Website NAP matching place page NAP (name, area, phone)

These are the strongest factors. If you want to rank high in the local search results, all you have to do is ensure your website and place page have more of these features than competitors currently ranking for your target keywords.

For a complete breakdown of the local SEO ranking factors, visit the below link, where one of the world's leading authorities on local SEO publishes an industry survey on the local ranking factors every year.

David Mihm's Local Search Ranking Factors
http://www.davidmihm.com/local-search-ranking-factors.shtml

Getting started with Local SEO

To get started, the first step is to create your business page on Google+. Visit the URL below, and complete every area of your profile as possible. This means creating a detailed description of your business, uploading as many photos as you can, listing trading hours, payment methods you accept, and so on. The more information you complete in your profile, the more you increase your chances of Google ranking your page higher.

Google+ for Businesses
http://www.google.com/+/business/

When creating your business listing, make sure you choose the correct category you want your business listing to appear in, e.g. if you provide plumbing as a service, you want to choose 'plumbing' as your category, not 'trades' or 'home repairs'.

Building citations

Citations are the links of local SEO. A citation occurs each time your name, address, phone number (NAP) is mentioned on the web. The more citations you have than your competitors, the more likely your site will rank higher than theirs. The easiest places to build citations are the many local business directories available for businesses.

Visit the below list from the LocalSEOGuide.com for a more comprehensive list of local business directories.

55 largest local business directories in the US

http://www.localseoguide.com/best-local-business-directories-seo/

Building reviews

Citations and reviews are the linkbuilding of local SEO. If you are only building citations, you only have half of the equation covered. To rank highly, you need to be aggressive in ensuring your business accumulates online reviews.

Many businesses struggle with this. This is because it's tough to get customers to fill out reviews!

You have to make it easy for your customers. If you make it easy for your customers to fill out reviews, you will get more reviews.

Include links to your business Google+ page on your website, email signatures, flyers, and business cards, prompting customers to leave a review. Encourage customers at the end of each job to leave a review. By creating every opportunity possible for customers to leave a review, you can significantly increase the amount of reviews you receive.

But whatever you do, do not buy reviews. This is a quick way to get into Google's dirty books. Purchased reviews are often picked up by Google's filters and not included on the profile.

The new meta: Microformats, Microdata, schema.org & Facebook Open Graph

Microformats, RDFa, microdata & schema.org. Where to start?

A growing problem emerged in the Internet in the past couple of years. There's literally billions of websites and webpages with an infinite amount of information — all completely unorganized... A bureaucratic nightmare!

There are endless pages about movies, customer reviews, local businesses, product catalogs, and so on, and there has been no standardized way of organizing or presenting this information.

A need emerged for a universal method to make it easy for search engines to quickly recognize this information.

Hence the birth of 'meta data' or 'semantic data' markup — new technologies that can be used on your site making it easier for search engines — and other technologies — to crawl, recognize and present your content to Internet users.

Considering banging your head against the wall, wondering why you're reading such a soul-destroyingly dry topic? Well, don't throw this book or your kindle out the window just yet...

These new technologies mean you can have greater control over your search listings, make it easier for search engines to crawl your site, and achieve 'rich snippets' like the example below, with which you can achieve higher click-through-rates and get more eyeballs on your content. Think of this new technology like meta description tags on steriods. Sound good?

Slipknot Tickets | **Slipknot Concert** Tickets & Tour Dates ...
www.ticketmaster.com › ... › Hard Rock/Metal ▾ Ticketmaster ▾
Results 1 - 10 of 21 - Buy Slipknot tickets from the official Ticketmaster.com site. Find **Slipknot tour** schedule, concert details, reviews and photos.

Sat, Oct 25	KNOTFEST - SATURDAY ...	San Manuel Amphitheater ...
Sat, Oct 25	Knotfest - 2 Day Pass	San Manuel Amphitheater ...
Sun, Oct 26	KNOTFEST - SUNDAY Single ...	San Manuel Amphitheater ...

Why use schema.org

So now we know what we can do with this new technology, where do we start? As always with new technologies, there's an ongoing debate about the best to use — RDFa, microdata, hCards, microformats, the list goes on...

Well I won't waste your time.

Google, Yahoo and Bing joined together in 2011 to hit the data nail on the head and created a standardized approach with schema.org – a reference site for the Microdata markup technology, which allows you to cover all of your meta-data needs.

Google openly stated that Microdata, and sister-website schema.org, is their preferred technology, and made it very clear not to mix 'meta data' technologies – fear of confusing their spider.

We're here for high rankings and traffic, not a lengthy debate on each individual technology, so let's go with what Google recommends for the purposes of this book.

If you want to read up on Google's thoughts on the above, and structured data, check out the article below.

About rich snippets and structured data
https://support.google.com/webmasters/answer/99170?hl=en

How to use schema.org

Google supports the below custom listings in the search results. If you have any of the below, your website can benefit from use of schema.org's recommended additional markup for your site.

- Reviews
- People
- Products
- Businesses and Organizations

- Recipes
- Events
- Music
- Video content

We'll use an example of a business listing to see how it might normally be coded, compared to following schema.org's recommendation.

Standard code for business details

```
<h1>Beachwalk Beachwear & Giftware</h1>
<p>A superb collection of fine gifts and clothing to accent
your stay in Mexico Beach.</p>
<p>3102 Highway 98</p>
<p>Mexico Beach, FL</p>
<p>Phone: 850-648-4200</p>
```

Microdata formatted code for business details

```
<div itemscope
itemtype="http://schema.org/LocalBusiness">
  <h1><span itemprop="name">Beachwalk Beachwear &
Giftware</span></h1>
  <span itemprop="description"> A superb collection of
fine gifts and clothing
  to accent your stay in Mexico Beach.</span>
  <div itemprop="address" itemscope
itemtype="http://schema.org/PostalAddress">
    <span itemprop="streetAddress">3102 Highway
98</span>
    <span itemprop="addressLocality">Mexico
Beach</span>,
```

```
<span itemprop="addressRegion">FL<
</div>
Phone: <span itemprop="telephone">8[
4200</span>
</div>
```

You can see how the above code gives the search engine a friendly nudge to recognize the information as a business listing.

While the above example will be just enough if you have a simple business listing, if you have any of the earlier-mentioned types of information on your site, you'll have to log on to schema.org to follow their documentation to ensure your data is correctly formatted.

Schema.org
http://schema.org

Facebook Open Graph

While we know schema.org is the best approach for adding meta data to your website, there is one additional 'meta data' technology you should also use...

Facebook's Open Graph language allows you to determine how your website listing appears when it is shared on Facebook.

If you do not include Facebook's Open Graph code on your site, when a user shares your content on Facebook it will show a plain listing on the news feed, with the responsibility on the user to describe the article and make it worth reading. If you include Facebook Open Graph code, it comes up looking sexy, just like your search listings if you have been using your meta title and meta description tags correctly.

By putting your best foot forward and making your listing show up correctly on Facebook, you will encourage more customers to click to your site, and increase the amount of likes and shares of your page. This will increase the social signals of the page.

Here's an example of properly formatted meta code using Facebook Open Graph. As you can see, there are only minor tweaks required to make your page show up nicely on Facebook's news feed... So go ahead and use it on your site!

```
<title>Buy Baseball Jackets Online</title>
<meta property='og:type' content='website'>
<meta property-'og:description' name='description'
content='Wide range of Baseball Jackets online, for all
leagues and players. Free delivery and free returns both-
ways in USA.' />
```

If you're worried about confusing search engines by using several 'structured data' technologies at the same time, such as Open Graph and schema.org, you won't have any problems.

Facebook Open Graph is mainly used by Facebook's web crawler, not by search engines, so you can use Open Graph and schema.org in tandem without any problems.

If you want to read up further on Facebook's Open Graph or have complex types of listings on your website, checkout Facebook's Open Graph guide below.

Open Graph Protocol
http://ogp.me/

Powerful SEO tools

There are many powerful SEO tools available that can help save hours, days or even weeks of your time.

The following tools can help find link building opportunities, diagnose website issues, create easy to understand SEO reports, make Google crawl your site faster and much much more. More often than not, one of the below tools will provide the information you need to achieve high rankings.

Are there more SEO tools out there than in this list? Sure. SEO tools are a dime a dozen. The following is a selection of the best tools I have found most useful over the years. Some are free, some are paid, but most at the very least offer a free trial—usually more than enough to start optimizing your web site for top rankings. So jump in and have fun.

Google Adwords Keyword Planner. Free.
http://www.google.com.au/intl/en/adwords/

The Google Adwords Keyword Planner has been mentioned several times throughout this book and for good reason. It's essential for every SEO project. With the Google Adwords Keyword Planner you can see how many times a keyword has been searched in Google and narrow this down by Country and even device type, such as mobile phones and so on.

This is essential for every SEO project to know how many times your keyword is being searched in Google.

Google Webmaster Tools. Free
https://www.google.com/webmasters/tools/home?hl=en

Google Webmaster Tools is another great tool, and if you haven't got Google Webmaster Tools set up, drop what you are doing and set it up now!

Google Webmaster Tools will report urgent messages if there are any severe problems when Google comes along and crawls your site. You can also submit your sitemap directly to Google from within Webmaster Tools, meaning you know Google has been given a friendly nudge to come around and pick up all the content on your website. This is a must have SEO tool for every site.

Open Site Explorer. Free for limited access. $99 per month for pro users.
http://www.opensiteexplorer.org/

Open Site Explorer is a must for understanding the links pointing to your site and competitor's web sites. Cheeky little tricks with Open Site Explorer include exporting your competitors' backlinks and looking over these links for opportunities to build links to your website.

Raven Tools. Free for one month. $99 per month for pro users.
http://raventools.com/tools/

Raven tools is great for getting a bird's eye view of how well the overall optimization of your website is faring with Google.

With Raven tools you can track link building campaigns, analyze competitor's websites, monitor social media, create automated SEO performance reports, and much much more.

Majestic SEO Site Explorer. Free to start. £29.99 for pro plan.
http://www.majesticseo.com/

Majestic SEO Site Explorer is a lesser known, but powerful link analysis tool.

Majestic's Site Explorer allows you to download historical reports of links built to a site, so you can see the historic patterns behind a website's link building.

Majestic SEO also has a very powerful tool called the Keyword Checker. The Keyword Checker allows you to analyze the competition for specific keywords, so you can know how difficult it will be to rank high enough for particular keywords.

Tools Pingdom. Free.
http://tools.pingdom.com/fpt/

Pingdom search tools is a great tool for monitoring how fast your website is loading, and finding opportunities to make it load even faster.

With the Pingdom Speed test you can see how fast your website loads, and how large the files are on your site. You can easily find the large files on your site that are chewing up resources and bloating your load time.

Pingdom also offer a really nifty service to monitor your website uptime and send you a text message and email alert whenever your server experiences problems and goes down for whatever reason. You can find out before anybody else and jump on your web hosting provider and ask them to fix any problems, before you lose too much traffic!

SEOBook Keyword Analyzer. Free.
http://tools.seobook.com/general/keyword-density/

By simply entering the URL to any page on your website, you can see a chart of the most optimized keywords on the page. This is great for getting a visual indication of keywords search engines are likely to pick up on the page.

SEOQuake. Free.
http://www.seoquake.com/

The SEOQuake toolbar gives you a powerful set of stats for any site you visit, right within your browser.

SEOQuake also has a great option that gives you the important stats for pages ranking in Google's search results. A great tool for snooping on competitors and doing market research.

SEOQuake's powerful toolbar works on Google Chrome, Safari & Firefox.

Authority Labs. Free to start. $99 per month for pro users.
http://authoritylabs.com/tour/

Authority Labs is a great tool for tracking your rankings in search engines. You can also track competitor's rankings too. Monitoring your rankings is a must for every SEO project, so you can measure improvements or trends over time.

XML Sitemaps. Free to trial. $19.99 for large sites.
http://www.xml-sitemaps.com/

XML Sitemaps is a fantastic tool for creating an XML sitemap to submit to Google.

The tool automatically formats the sitemap so it is in the right format for Google and other search engines. With XML Sitemaps you can create a sitemap for your website within minutes.

Google Snippet Optimization Tool. Free.
http://www.seomofo.com/snippet-optimizer.html

This handy little tool lets you type out title tags and meta tags and see a live preview of how your site will appear in the search engines.

Ontolo. $47 per month.
http://ontolo.com/

Ontolo is a goldmine for broken linkbuilding, making it very easy to filter through the many broken link opportunities out there so you can reach out and start building links.

Buzzstream. Free trial. $19 per month for regular use.
http://www.buzzstream.com/link-building/plans-pricing#features

Buzzstream helps you find broken linkbuilding opportunities and track your linkbuilding outreach efforts. Buzzstream will even find the contact details on the web site for you. Can be used as an alternative to Ontolo.

Google Page Speed Insights. Free.
https://developers.google.com/speed/pagespeed/insights

Google Page Speed Insights is a fantastic tool provided by Google to help speed up your website. Google Page Speed Insights will give you a score on how well your load time is performing, and provides a simple set of suggestions to forward to your developers and speed up your site.

Traffic Travis. Free for beginners. $97 once off for Pro users.
http://www.traffictravis.com/

Traffic Travis is a great and simple SEO overview tool. Unlike many of the other tools listed, Traffic Travis is a downloadable tool you must download to your desktop (PCs only!).

Traffic Travis provides SEO health checks, competitor analysis, ranking tracking, linkbuilding research, and much more.

Google Trends. Free.
http://www.google.com/trends/?hl=en

Google Trends provides powerful stats of search trends over time. Great for seeing how your market performs overall, and how demand changes over time for your keywords.

Google Alerts. Free.
http://www.google.com.au/alerts

Google Alerts is great for keeping an eye out for fresh new search results in Google.

You can put in any search term, add your email address, and Google Alerts will send you an email each time a new listing appears in Google's search results.

Great for monitoring new links pointing to your site, mentions of your brand, and new content indexed by Google — so you can reach out and build links or add comments.

Market Samurai. Free to start. $147 for pro users. http://www.marketsamurai.com/

Market Samurai is one of those reliable tools that have been around in the SEO industry for many, many years.

The favorite keyword research tool of many SEO gurus, Market Samurai is powerful for generating ideas for keywords and analyzing keywords for competitiveness — so you can uncover the keywords you can target for easy rankings.

Redirect Checker. Free. http://www.seologic.com/webmaster-tools/url-redirect

If you have ever setup a URL redirect — or asked your developer to — it's always a good idea to check and ensure the redirect has been setup correctly.

Use the redirect checker to make sure your redirects are returning successful responses to the web browser, so you can feel confident Google is picking it up properly too!

SEO Browser. Free

http://seo-browser.com/

Takes a webpage or website, and shows you what it looks like to a search engine, without graphics and layout. This is a fantastic tool for getting a birds eye view of what Google is going to pick up on your site.

Moz. Free and Paid.
http://moz.com/tools

No book on SEO would ever be complete without a mention of Moz (formerly SEOMOZ). Moz offer brand monitoring, rankings tracking, on-page SEO grading, search engine crawl tests and much more. An essential toolbox for every SEO practitioner, from beginner to advanced.

Robots.txt Checker. Free.
http://www.frobee.com/robots-txt-check

Many robots.txt files can often have slight errors that are difficult to pick up, especially for larger sites. Run your robots.txt file through this tool for a free analysis to see if there are any errors.

Xenu's Link Sleuth. Free
http://home.snafu.de/tilman/xenulink.html

Don't be put off by the old-school design on the page that offers this very powerful SEO-tool for free.

Xenu's Link Sleuth is one of the most powerful SEO-tools available, that will crawl your entire website, or a list of links, and offer very powerful and juicy stats for each of your pages, such as stats on which pages have 404 errors, 301 redirects, server errors, title tags, meta desc tags, the list goes on! This tool has been around for years, and is a must-have tool for the more advanced SEO practitioner.

Robots.txt Generator. Free
http://www.yellowpipe.com/yis/tools/robots.txt/

If you're lazy like I am, you'll love this free robots.txt generator. Works great for the most basic or advanced robots.txt needs.

Schema Creator. Free
http://schema-creator.org/

Great and easy-to-use tool to automatically generate your schema.org markup.

Ubersuggest. Free.
http://ubersuggest.org/

Automatically download the auto-suggested keywords from Google's search results for a nice, juicy collection of long-tail keywords.

Everything You Need to Know About Penguin 2.0 & Hummingbird

On May 22nd, 2013 Google's head of web spam, Matt Cutts, announced the next big update affecting sites appearing in the search results. This update is called Penguin 2.0.

After Google's history of releasing game changing updates, this update had been anticipated, even feared, by many members of the SEO community.

And for good reason. The updates released in previous years have caused entire websites to drop completely out of Google, and many webmasters and SEOs were forced to change their entire approach to marketing their business.

Here's what Matt Cutts posted on his blog:

We started rolling out the next generation of the Penguin webspam algorithm this afternoon (May 22, 2013), and the rollout is now complete. About 2.3% of English-US queries are affected to the degree that a regular user might notice. The change has also finished rolling out for other languages world-wide. The scope of Penguin varies by language, e.g. languages with more webspam will see more impact.

Why you should keep a cool head about Penguin 2.0

Penguin has been anticipated by Google and the SEO community as a game-changing update. However, many members of the SEO community haven't been affected by this update at all. Why is this so?

The update is a more widespread version of the first Penguin update. Bad practices that Penguin 1.0 and Penguin 2.0 penalizes, such as overly spammy anchor text, and links from low quality websites, have not been widely used or supported by the SEO community for the past 12-months.

This update is much more likely to affect very low quality, spam-related websites that are using outdated 'black-hat' tactics.

If you have been following the link building best practices outlined in this book, you can breathe a sigh of relief — it's unlikely you will have been negatively affected by this update.

What Does Penguin 2.0 Target?

Google never fully reveals the inner workings of their updates, otherwise Google would be making it easier for the evil spammers to fill up the search results with low quality pages. That said, we can piece together reports from Google and the SEO Community to create a fairly clear picture of what this update targets.

Matt Cutts has publicly said the Penguin 2.0 update is further devaluing web spam and suspicious links pointing to websites. So we know the update is focused on low quality links.

An online study by the industry authority Search Engine Watch revealed sites affected by the Penguin 2.0 update typically had 66% targeted keywords in their links pointing to the page, while healthy sites in the top-10 had targeted keywords making up no more than 29% of the links pointing to a particular page. The lessons learned from the first Penguin update still remain true. Your target keyword text should not take up more than 20-30% of the links pointing to a page.

Google have also mentioned that this update should affect industries differently. The below study by Mozcast.com reveals how much the rankings have changed across the different industries. A higher temperature in the list indicates the rankings are moving around considerably.

The first temperature listed is the temperature (volatility) of the rankings after the update, and the second temperature is the volatility of the rankings before the update. A higher % change means the industry has been heavily affected by this update.

- 33.0% (80°/60°) – Retailers & General Merchandise
- 31.2% (81°/62°) – Real Estate
- 30.8% (90°/69°) – Dining & Nightlife
- 29.1% (89°/69°) – Internet & Telecom
- 26.0% (82°/65°) – Law & Government
- 24.4% (79°/64°) – Finance
- 23.5% (81°/65°) – Occasions & Gifts
- 20.8% (88°/73°) – Beauty & Personal Care
- 17.3% (70°/60°) – Travel & Tourism
- 15.7% (87°/75°) – Vehicles
- 15.5% (84°/73°) – Arts & Entertainment
- 15.4% (72°/62°) – Health
- 15.0% (83°/72°) – Home & Garden
- 14.2% (78°/69°) – Family & Community
- 13.4% (79°/70°) – Apparel
- 13.1% (78°/69°) – Hobbies & Leisure
- 12.0% (74°/66°) – Jobs & Education
- 11.5% (88°/79°) – Sports & Fitness
- 7.8% (75°/70°) – Food & Groceries
- -3.7% (70°/73°) – Computers & Electronics

What to do about Penguin 2.0

Whatever you do, don't lose your mind and start making drastic changes on your website. It's very likely your site has weathered the storm, or if you have noticed some slight changes—it's also likely you are experiencing normal ranking movements.

If you are concerned or have reason to believe your website has been affected by this update, progress through the following steps and you can identify the cause and make appropriate action steps.

1. Check your rankings and traffic around the 20th of May, 2012. Have you noticed any clear decreases in traffic, visits from particular keywords, or movement in rankings?

2. If you have noticed any of these decreases, identify the pages that will have been affected, and look up the pages' back-link information in Open Site Explorer (opensiteexplorer.org) or Majestic SEO (majesticseo.com). Do these pages have suspicious amounts of over-optimized, saturated anchor text pointing to the page, or a large amount of low quality sites linking to the page?

3. If you have noticed a decrease around the 22nd of May, 2012 and have confirmed there are spammy links pointing to the page, follow the steps in the chapter on troubleshooting common SEO problems. The steps are the same for Penguin 2.0 penalties.

If your website is not showing any of the above warning signs, it's likely you have weathered the storm.

What you need to know about the Hummingbird update

With a habit of surprising search engine marketers and businesses with gigantic updates, on September, 26th 2013 Google announced the biggest update to their core algorithm.

Titled 'Hummingbird', this major update was a total overhaul of Google's algorithm that determines which search results are the most relevant to the user. This update focused on improving the ability for the algorithm to better understand the intent behind a user's search. Google's talented technical gurus achieved this by improving the technology that understands the contextual terms in a search query.

For example, if you searched for 'where to buy an iPhone 5', which this new algorithm Google should be able to understand you're looking for a location near your home to buy an iPhone.

Google search chief Amit Singhal stated 'Hummingbird is the first major update of it's type since 2001'. At the same conference, Matt Cutts reported that Google was using the algorithm for a month before it was even announced, and no one even noticed!

So you might be wondering how this affects you...

Keep on creating the best, highest-quality content as you should be already. Make your pages relevant to the user. This was not an update targeting link building or spammers. With the Hummingbird update, it's business as usual.

Bonus chapter: Google's 2014 & 2015 algorithm updates

Some might say the 2014 and 2015 Google algorithm updates were less severe than previous years. The recent Google updates have largely affected large brands or sites using extremely spammy SEO tactics.

That said, if you want to be successful, you need to be well informed on the latest updates to make sure your site doesn't trigger any of Google's spam filters. In some cases, you can take advantage of the updates to the algorithm and get even higher rankings.

Listed below are the major updates to be aware of.

Panda 4.0

On May 20, 2014 Matt Cutts, the head of Google's web spam team — the team that release the majority of updates to Google's algorithm — confirmed Google were rolling out another major update.

Reports from SEO professionals and webmasters confirmed this was an update targeting large websites and brands using scraped or copied content. Sites such as ask.com and ebay.com are examples of sites affected. These sites were penalized for the below areas:

- Poor User Experience
- Scraped Content

The above definitions are somewhat vague, making it hard to confirm if you have been affected by the Panda update.

To identify a penalty from this update, below are some questions to ask:

- Is there a visible drop-off in search engine traffic starting around late May this year?

- Does my website scrape large amounts of contents from other websites?

- Does my website create a large amount of pages with duplicate content, or pages with light content, creating a poor user experience?

If the answer to all questions is no, give yourself a pat on the back. You have nothing to worry about.

If the answer to any of the above is yes, the below excerpt by one of the leading bloggers covering Panda 4.0, Glenn Gabe, sums up the causes and affects nicely, or not so nicely if you've been a victim...

"If you anger users, provide a horrible user experience, present low-quality content, or deceive them in any way, the mighty Panda may pounce. Google can pick up when users are unhappy, and if that happens enough, you could be heading down a very dangerous path Panda-wise."

While there is no official guideline from Google on how to recover from a penalty from this update, below is a straightforward treatment plan if you're visibly affected and need to work on recovering your rankings.

Important: Only proceed through the below if it is very clear you've been affected by this update. It is recommended you confirm with an experienced SEO professional you have been affected before proceeding with any of the below steps.

- Remove any widgets or scripts using scraped content.
- Delete any sections with a high amount of duplicated content.
- Alternatively, use no-index and no-follow meta tags to block sections filled with duplicate content from search engines. Or use rel=canonical tags on duplicate pages to point search engines to the canonical page.
- If you have a large amount of ads pushing your content below-the-fold, you may have to rearrange the ads on your site so your content appears above-the-fold, and you provide a more positive experience for users.

To read up further, the below articles cover Panda 4.0 at great length.

Panda 4.0 Analysis

http://www.hmtweb.com/marketing-blog/panda-4-analysis/

Google's 4.0 Update, A Quick Primer
http://www.business2community.com/seo/googles-panda-4-0-update-quick-primer-0917808#!bHoJ98

Panda 4.0 Help
http://searchenginewatch.com/article/2353139/Panda-4.0-Help-Google-Clarifies-Tremors-3-Analogies-for-Diagnosing-Hits

Authorship Photo Drop

You may remember Google+ profile photos appearing alongside articles and listings in the Google search results.

Well now these listings have become a relic of the past.

On June 26th, Google's trends analyst, John Mueller, announced to the world that Google will remove all author photos and Google+ view and subscriber counts from the Google search results, with the aim of providing a more consistent experience across devices.

Shortly thereafter the photos were dropped from the search results, with the exception of the 'Google News' search results.

Does this mean you shouldn't be making use of Google's authorship by linking up your Google+ profile with content or articles you publish online?

Not necessarily. While the photos no longer appear in the results, the ranking factors have not been affected by this update.

In fact, if you are regularly publishing blog posts or articles, you should verify your authorship with your Google+ account following the instructions from the below article. This will allow you to take advantage of the positive ranking factors resulting from verified authorship.

Author Information in Search Results
https://support.google.com/webmasters/answer/1408986

Google Announces the End of Author Photos in Search: What You Should Know
http://moz.com/blog/bye-bye-author-pics

Pigeon

On July 24th Google confirmed the release of a new algorithm update called 'Pigeon', sending the SEO community into a flutter...

This was an algorithmic update, and not a penalty-based update, targeting local search results. This means no penalties were introduced. What has been affected are the parts of Google's algorithm that determine how local listings appear high or low, and how often the local listings appear at all.

The three major impacts of this update are listed below, with suggestions on what to do if you have been affected.

1) Local rankings are increasingly affected by domain authority.

Suggestion: If you have local listings in Google and noticed a decrease in ranking position, it's time to start working on building the amount of quality links pointing to your website.

2) Local listings disappearing for a large amount of keywords.

Suggestion: If you were depending on local search results, and the local results are no longer showing up for your keywords, start working on acquiring organic non-local rankings, and maybe even considering a pay-per-click campaign while you are waiting for your new rankings to build up.

3) Large directories such as Yelp, Urbanspoon, Tripadvisor and Booking.com receiving higher rankings.

Suggestion: If your competitor's listings on these major directories are ranking for your local keywords, you may want to confirm your existing lists on the major business directories. You may even want to consider building links to your directory listing to overtake your competitor's positions.

This update has been considered a major update, but like the earlier Panda update this year, many honest businesses have coasted through unscathed, which is a relief.

If you want to read up further on the online coverage surrounding Pigeon, some great articles on the subject are listed below.

Experts Weigh In On Google's "Pigeon" Update Aimed At Improving Local Search Results
http://searchengineland.com/experts-weigh-googles-pigeonlocal-search-algorithm-update-198499

Google Launches New Pigeon Update — How Does It Affect Your Website
http://www.link-assistant.com/news/google-pigeon-update.html

Worried About Pigeon? Just Keep On Truckin'
http://searchengineland.com/worried-pigeon-just-keep-truckin-200219

HTTPS/SSL update

On August 26th, 2014 Google confirmed they started using HTTPS as a ranking signal. Albeit a minor signal, affecting less than 1% of searches.... For now.

Google openly admitted this is part of a long-term initiative to encourage the majority of site-owners to move over to using SSL to secure their websites.

Words on this straight from the horses mouth:

"Over time, we may decide to strengthen it, because we'd like to encourage all website owners to switch from HTTP to HTTPS to keep everyone safe on the web."

Retrieved from 'HTTPS as a ranking signal' - Google Webmaster Central Blog http://googlewebmastercentral.blogspot.com.au/2014/08/https-as-ranking-signal.html

Does this mean you should rush out and change over your entire site to HTTPS right now?

Not necessarily...

Migrating or reconfiguring your website address is a substantial undertaking, and only recommended for experienced SEO professionals and web developers.

Google may be considering making HTTP a stronger ranking factor in the future — but they haven't done it yet.

If you administer a large website, it may be worth speaking with your developer on what's required to install an SSL certificate on your website, so you can begin planning the infrastructure required to make this happen in future.

If you do move your website across to use HTTPS as the default method of accessing your site, you and your developer should read the below guide by Google in detail before making any changes.

But it's not recommended to go through this change unless absolutely necessary, until more information has been released by Google and the SEO community.

Move A Site With URL Changes
https://support.google.com/webmasters/answer/603308
5?hl=en&ref_topic=6033084

Panda 4.0, 2014

On September 23rd, Google announced another major release to the Panda update, targeting pages with a poor user experience, or pages with thin or extremely poor content.

Like all Google updates, Google's description is painfully vague and mysterious. Thankfully, the SEO community have already analyzed this update at great length and detailed their findings online.

Sites negatively affected by this update:
- Sites extremely thin or light content, such as pages with blank or empty content.
- Pages loaded with a large amount of affiliate links stuffed into the content.
- Pages with a large amount of keyword stuffing on the page.
- Pages with deceptive ad tactics, such as text link ads used in key navigation areas in order to 'trick users' to click on the ads.

In other words, pages that create a horrible experience for users have been affected. The type of pages Google obviously doesn't want ranking at the top of search.

This update can is actually a blessing in disguise. Many site owners have reported they are seeing an rise in rankings and traffic. Google themselves have reported that this update will result in many small to medium websites with high quality content rising to the top.

These are the type of site owners ensuring content on their site is high quality, and they are creating a positive user experience for visitors.

It's likely you haven't seen any changes due to this update if you haven't been using the tactics described above. If you have seen changes in rankings or traffic around the 23rd of September, you may want to read the below articles for further detailed findings covering Panda 4.1.

Panda Update Rolling Out
https://plus.google.com/+PierreFar/posts/7CWs3a3yoeY

Panda 4.1 Analysis and Findings
http://www.hmtweb.com/marketing-blog/panda-4-1-analysis/

Your Guide to Google's Panda 4.1 Algorithm
http://www.huffingtonpost.com/jayson-demers/your-guide-to-googles-pan_b_5959634.html

Penguin 3.0

On Friday October 17th, 2014 Google announced the latest algorithm refresh titled 'Penguin 3.0'.

Like previous Penguin updates, this update is focused on low quality links. This update is also focused on relieving penalties for site owners who cleaned up their low quality link building in the past, and submitted a reconsideration request to Google.

At the writing of this book, there's few specifics published, besides Google stating it targets 'poor quality links'. Google are tight-lipped with the details on how their algorithm works as always.

But the good news is, overall, very few webmasters reported any issues. Look over your rankings and search traffic around October 17th. If you can't see any obvious trends, then it's likely you haven't been affected at all. If you notice any very steep declines in rankings or traffic around this date, then it's possible you have been affected and should look into it further.

If you have been creating high quality links, and stayed away from spammy tactics like keyword stuffing, articles written in poor english, or spammy links built on low quality sites, give yourself a cocktail and a pat on the back — there's nothing to worry about and it's time to get back to getting more rankings.

Key areas of note
- Penguin 3.0 is a worldwide refresh, affecting all countries.

- The refresh is spanning a few weeks onwards from October, 17th.
- Impacts less than 1% of English queries.
- Pierre Far from Google's specified this is a 'refresh' not an update. Historically, refreshes are less severe and affect less sites.

If you're a resource junky and dying to read up further, check out the below resources.

See updates as they are reported - Google PageRank & Google Updates, Search Engine Round Table
https://www.seroundtable.com/category/google-updates

Google Releases Penguin 3.0
http://searchengineland.com/google-releases-first-penguin-update-year-206169

Monitor the latest chatter on Penguin 3.0 on Google+
https://plus.google.com/s/%23penguin

Penguin 3.0: The Definitive Guide to Diagnosis and Recovery
http://www.forbes.com/sites/jaysondemers/2014/10/20/penguin-3-0-the-definitive-guide-to-diagnosis-and-recovery/

Mobile Algorithm Update April, 2015

On February 26th, 2015 Google announced a game changing update for the SEO industry. On the 21st of April, 2015 websites with solid mobile support will rank higher in search results for mobile users. Websites with no mobile support will not rank highly in mobile search results.

Whether we like it or not, mobile users are here to stay. And whether we like it or not, Google are driving the mobile revolution. With the largest mobile app store in the world, largest mobile operating system in the world, and largest amount of mobile search users, it's easy to see why mobile users are a priority for Google.

Google are rolling out this update to give webmasters a nudge to make the Internet more user-friendly for mobile users. If you are not supporting mobile users, it's time to start seriously thinking about increasing your mobile support, not only for better search engine results, but for better sales and conversions — it's likely a very large segment of your traffic are mobile users.

If you are concerned about your rankings for searches performed on desktop and laptop machines you have nothing to worry about. Google has made it very clear this mobile friendly update will only affect search results on mobile devices.

What to do about the mobile update.

If you want to increase your support for mobile devices and be more search engine friendly, you have three options...

1. Create a responsive website.
Responsive websites are the cream of the crop when it comes to websites that support both desktop and mobile devices. With responsive websites, both mobile and desktop users see the same pages and same content, and everything is automatically sized to fit the screen. It's becoming more and more common for WordPress templates and new websites to feature a responsive layout.

2. Dynamically serve different content to mobile and desktop users.
You can ask your web developer to detect which devices are accessing your website and automatically deliver a different version of your site catered to the device. This is a more complimented setup better suited for very large sites with thousands of pages, when a responsive approach is not practical.

3. Host your mobile content on a separate subdomain, example m.yourwebsite.com
While Google have stated they support this implementation, I recommend against it. You need a lot of redirects in place and jump through giant hoops to ensure search engines are recognizing your special mobile subdomain as a copy of your main site. Responsive websites are popular for good reason, it's much easier and cheaper to maintain one website, rather than additionally having to maintain a mobile copy of your website on a mobile subdomain.

Google have stated that this mobile update is going to be fairly straightforward. Either your website supports mobile devices or it doesn't. Google will not reward websites with better mobile support with higher rankings over websites with average mobile support—for now. If your site supports mobile devices, you can rest assured you will most likely be fine with this update. Run your website quickly through the below tool and see if your website supports mobile devices in Google's eyes...

Mobile Friendly Test Tool
https://www.google.com/webmasters/tools/mobile-friendly/

The technical details of building a responsive website are well beyond the scope of this book, and would fill an entire book. That said, mobile SEO can be ridiculously simple.

If you have a responsive website that delivers the same content to mobile and desktop users, automatically resizes content to the screen, and is user friendly, all you have to do is follow the SEO recommendations in this book, and your mobile results will be top notch from an SEO perspective.

For guidelines direct from the horse's mouth, so to speak, you can read Google's mobile support documentation for webmasters and web developers.

Mobile Friendly Websites

https://developers.google.com/webmasters/mobile-sites/

If you want to read up on some of the blog coverage on this update, check out the below resources...

Finding More Mobile Friendly Search Results
http://googlewebmastercentral.blogspot.com/2015/02/finding-more-mobile-friendly-search.html

9 Things About Google's Mobile Friendly Update
http://moz.com/blog/9-things-about-googles-mobile-friendly-update

Keep up to date with Google's 2015 updates

As of the last couple of years, the Google updates have become progressively frequent, with a change to the algorithm witnessed and reported on every month or so.

If you want to stay ahead of the curve, and save yourself a nasty shock from an unexpected update, remember the below resources are great starting points to stay informed.

If there is a significant update to Google's algorithm, it will be covered on at least one of the below pages.

Google Algorithm Change History
http://moz.com/google-algorithm-change

Google Webmaster Central Blog
http://googlewebmastercentral.blogspot.com

Google PageRank & Algorithm Updates
https://www.seroundtable.com/category/google-updates

Bonus chapter: The quick and dirty guide to pay-per-click advertising with Google AdWords

Why bother with pay-per-click advertising?

You would have to be as crazy as a box of weasels to pay each time someone visits your site with pay-per-click advertising, when you can rank high in Google for free... Right?

Not necessarily.

Pay-per-click advertising has certain advantages over SEO.

With pay-per-click you can:

- Send customers to your website within hours, not the months it takes for solid SEO results.

- Track results down to the penny, and get very clear insights into the financial performance of your advertising. Simply set up conversion tracking with the instructions provided by Google, or whichever pay-per-click provider you choose.

- Achieve a much larger overall number of customers to your website by running pay-per-click in tandem with your other marketing efforts.

- Achieve a positive financial return on your marketing spend in many cases, and keep on selling to these customers in the future.

There is one caveat to the last point.

If you are a small fish trying to enter an extremely competitive market, such as house loans, insurance or international plane flights, it's likely the big players in the market are buying a large amount of advertising, forcing the average cost-per-click to astronomical prices, and making it difficult for new players to get a profitable return...

If you're selling pizza delivery in New York, pool cleaning in Los Angeles, or cheap baseball jackets... In other words, if you're selling a common local trade, service, or product online, it's likely you can receive a profitable return on your advertising spend.

While pay-per-click really deserves its own book, this is a quick and dirty bonus chapter, jam-packed with just enough information to get a pay-per-click campaign setup, avoid common mistakes pay-per-click newbies make, and send more customers and sales to your business.

If you want to delve deeper into the science of pay-per-click advertising, I've included some great resources on AdWords at the end of the chapter.

Sound good? Let's get started.

Which is the best PPC provider to start with?

There's many pay-per-click providers out there, Google AdWords and BingAds are the two largest players.

Google AdWords is the perfect starting point. You can sell anything on Google AdWords if you have money to spend because the user base is so large.

If you're looking to jump into pay-per-click advertising, get started with Google AdWords. Move on to the other pay-per-click networks after you have some experience under your belt.

Some of the reasons AdWords is the best choice for your first foray into pay-per-click advertising:

- Fast, instant results. Send new customers to your site within an hour or two.

- Advanced targeting technology. Target users based on where they are located, or what browser or device they are using. Google's ad targeting technology is arguably the best in the world.

- With Google's search engine market share at 67 percent, and Bing at 18.7 percent, you can reach out to the largest potential amount of customers with Google.

- Due to the popularity of AdWords, there's a wealth of knowledge on the Internet on running AdWords campaigns successfully.

Ensuring success with research and a plan.

Like all marketing projects, for an AdWords campaign to be successful you need to start with research and a solid plan. Without first defining your goals, and designing a robust strategy to achieve them, it's impossible to create a successful marketing campaign — you'll have no way of determining if the outcome is successful!

Here are some important questions to ask yourself before you get started.

- What is the objective of the campaign? Sales, web enquiries, sign-ups, or branding?

- What is the maximum monthly budget you can afford?

- What is the maximum cost-per-enquiry, or cost-per-acquisition you can afford?

For example, if you are selling snow jackets at $100, and your profit margin is 20%... You really can't afford to spend much more than $20 on each customer you acquire. Write this figure down, and review it later. You may need to first run a small test campaign to determine if pay-per-click is profitable, and the right marketing channel for your business.

- What are the most common characteristics of your customers?

Typically, you can use the defining characteristics of your customers to create a laser-targeted campaign, which will increase its overall profitability.

For example, if you're selling late-night pizza delivery in New York, you don't want to be paying for the lovely folk in Idaho searching for late-night pizza delivery.

Write down as much of these common characteristics as you can, and in the settings recommendations, if there's an option to target these customers, I'll tell you how to do it.

How to choose the right kind of keywords

It's the moment you've been waiting for. The keywords! Precious keywords.

Just like SEO, getting your keywords right with AdWords is critical if you want a successful campaign.

Unlike SEO, with AdWords there are different types of keywords, called keyword match-types. I've listed the main keyword match types below.

Broad match keywords.

The default type of keywords all AdWords campaign use — if you don't change any settings — are Broad Match keywords. With Broad match keywords, Google will take any word out of your phrase, and serve up ads for searches hardly related to your phrase.

Needless to say, almost all new campaigns should NOT be using broad match keywords to start with. Have a look at the example below.

keyword:
tennis shoes

will trigger ads for:
designer shoes
dress shoes
basketball shoes
tennis bags
tennis equipment

Phrase match keywords.

Phrase match keywords will only show your ad for searches containing your core phrase. With phrase match keywords, you can exercise a higher level of control and purchase traffic from more relevant customers. And higher relevancy usually means more sales:

To enter a phrase match keyword, when adding keywords to your account wrap the keywords with "" quotation marks and these keywords will become broad-match keywords.

keyword:
"tennis shoes"

will trigger ads for:
tennis shoes
best tennis shoes
tennis shoes online

will not trigger ads for:
shoes tennis
tennis shoe
tennis sneakers
tennis players

Exact match keywords.

Exact match keywords will only trigger ads for the exact phrase you enter. Needless to say, with exact match keywords in your campaign you can have a high level of accuracy, and achieve more sales. Exact match keywords are indispensable for every AdWords campaign.

To enter exact match keywords, wrap the keywords with [] brackets when adding keywords to your account, they will become exact match keywords.

keyword:

[tennis shoes]

will trigger ads for:
tennis shoes

will not match for:
tennis shoe
tennis shoes online
best tennis shoes

Broad match modified keywords.

Broad match modified keywords are a special keyword allowing you to have both accuracy and a large amount of exposure. With broad match modified keywords, you will trigger ads that include a combination of all of the words in your phrase.

To create broad match modified keywords, add a + sign to the keywords when adding them to your account.

keyword:
+tennis +shoes

will match for:
where to buy tennis shoes online
tennis shoes
buy shoes for tennis
buy tennis shoes

will not match for:
tennis joggers
buy tennis shoe

margaret thatcher

Negative keywords

One of the most important, but easily overlooked keywords are negative keywords. Negative keywords will prevent your ads for showing for searches that include your negative keyword.

If you are using phrase match or any kind of broad match keyword, you should be using negative keywords. Negative keywords are vital for ensuring you are not paying for advertising for irrelevant searches.

Enter negative keywords in your campaign by adding a - minus sign in front of your keywords when adding keywords, or going to the 'shared library' on the left hand column in your AdWords account, and you can apply negative keywords across your entire account, a great time-saving tip.

keywords:
+car +service
-guide
-manual

will trigger ads for:
car service los angeles
car service mechanic
car service tips

will not trigger ads for:
free car service guide

ford mustang 65 car service manual

When choosing keywords, you need a balance between keywords with a high level of accuracy, such as exact match keywords, and keywords with a larger amount of reach, such as phrase match or broad match modified keywords.

Use a mix of the above keywords in your campaign, then review the performance of different keyword types after your campaign has been running, when you have some data.

Structuring your campaign with ad groups.

AdWords offer an excellent way of organizing your keywords called ad groups.

If you organize your campaign correctly, you can quickly see which areas of your campaign are profitable and not-so-profitable.

Fortunately, AdWords offers a very powerful way to structure your campaigns called ad groups.

Let's say you have a Harley Davidson dealership, with a wide range of HD gear from bikes to accessories and clothing, below is an example of ad groups you might create

- Harley Davidson motorbikes
- Harley Davidson parts
- Harley Davidson accessories

- Harley Davidson jackets

With ad groups you can:

- Create separate ads from the rest of your campaign. Great for testing.
- Have a select range of keywords, specific to the ad group.
- Set a specific bid for the ad group. Great if you have higher priced products or services you're willing to pay more for.
- Get detailed data on the performance of your ad groups

Structure your campaign with ad groups with a very clear and simple sense of organization when you setup your AdWords campaign. You'll get better insights into the performance of your campaign, and it will make your life easier when you want to make changes later on down-the-track.

How to crush the competition with killer AdWords ads

Writing a killer AdWords ad is essential to the success of your campaign. Poorly written AdWords ads can increase the overall costs of your campaign, sending less traffic to your website for more money.... We don't want that.

With your AdWords ads, you want to:

- Attract clicks from interested customers, not tire-kickers.
- Include keywords related to what the user searched for.
- Encourage a clear call to action and benefit for the user.

AdWords ads are made up of the following components.

1. Headline. Your headline has a maximum of 25 characters. With your headline, you should include the keyword the user is searching for, or capture the user's curiosity.

2. Description lines. You have two description lines at a maximum of 35 characters each. Your description lines should make it crystal clear what you are selling, the benefits of clicking through to your website, and a call-to-action, in other words, what you want the user to do.

3. Display URL. You have 35 characters for a custom URL that will be displayed to users in the search results. Display URLs are great as you can actually display a different URL to the user than the URL of the page they will arrive on. You can take advantage of this to encourage more users to arrive on your site.

I've listed below some winning ads so we can see why they are so successful...

Injured in an Accident?
www.1800needhelp.com/
You May Be Entitled to $10,000 +
Free Case Evaluation. 24/7 Call Us

Flowers Online - $19.99
www.fromyouflowers.com/
Delivered Today Beautiful & Fresh!
"Best Value Flowers" - CBS News

In each of the above, we can see some similarities. Each ad has:

- An interesting headline. Each ad captures the curiosity of the user, through use of special characters, asking a question or posting a competitive offer right in the headline.

- Clear benefits. Each ad has a compelling offer making the ad stand out from the search results, such as a no-risk, money back guarantee, same day delivery, or a free-evaluation.
- A clear call-to-action. The first two ads make it clear what the next step should be. In the third ad, the call-to-action is not explicit, but it is obvious. By having 'Online - $19.99' in the headline, and 'Delivered Today', it is clear the user can order flowers online to be delivered the same-day, if they click on the ad and visit the website.

If you want to read up in greater detail on successful AdWords ads and why they crush the competition, the below article is a good starting point.

11 successful ads and why they crush the competition
http://blog.crazyegg.com/2012/03/26/successful-
adwords-ads/

How much to pay for keywords

One of the most common burning questions for AdWords
newbies is... how much should I bid on my keywords?

The Google AdWords cost-per-click network uses a
bidding system, which means you are taking place in an
auction with competing advertisers. By increasing your
bids your ad position increases, leading to more traffic or
customers to your site.

Here is where it gets interesting. Google awards an
advantage to advertisers showing ads with high quality
and high relevancy. This is Google's Quality Score
technology. Ads with a higher amount of clicks and
relevancy are awarded a higher Quality Score, and receive
increased ad positions — at a cheaper price!

Keep this in mind when writing your ads and choosing
your keywords. Your ads should be relevant to achieve the
highest Quality Score possible, so you can receive the
cheapest cost-per-click.

There is no clear answer for predicting your ideal bid price
on the other hand. You should only pay for what you can
afford. You can find out how much you can afford by
doing some simple math.

For example, lets take the below scenario.

- You're selling video courses for $100.
- For every 100 visitors, 3 turn into customers. This is a conversion rate of 3%.
- If you spend $100 on AdWords, and achieve a $1 cost-per-click, you'll receive $300 in sales, and $200 in profit...

Here's the catch...

You can only find out what your cost-per-click is after running your campaign for a while, when you have accumulated some reliable data. So only run a small test campaign to begin with. Use the information you do have to make some projections, and only pay what you can afford.

Adwords Settings for Getting Started

The single most important factor in ensuring your campaign is successful is to fill out all of the settings when you setup your campaign. Whatever you do, do not rush through the campaign settings or leave them empty, otherwise you will end up paying for advertising to people who have no interest in what you're selling.

Got it? Good.

I've listed some recommended AdWords settings below for reference, but if you are not setting up your AdWords campaign right now, feel free to skip to the end of this chapter for some closing recommendations on reviewing AdWords campaigns for long-term success.

1. If you haven't already, create an account at http://adwords.google.com. When signing up, enter your Google account, or let the tool create one for you if you don't already have one.

2. Once fully signed in, click on the big button 'Create your first campaign'

Campaign name:
Enter a descriptive name for your campaign.

Type:
Choose 'search network only' from the drop-down. This is important. Make sure you select this option, unless you know what you are doing, otherwise you will also end up buying advertising on less relevant sites.

Select 'All features - All options for the Search Network, with Display Select'. Why would we want to restrict ourselves and give ourselves less options and features? Choose it, features are juicy. Trust me.

Networks:
Unselect 'include search partners'. We want to advertise on Google, not other smaller, potentially less-relevant websites.

Locations:

If you are targeting customers from a specific area, country, state or city, enter the most relevant setting for your customers here. Whatever you do, don't forget about this setting, otherwise if you're a local business you'll end up buying advertising half way around the world!

Bid strategy:
Choose 'I'll manually set my bids for clicks'. This allows you to make sure you are only setting cost-per-click bids you can afford, more on setting bids later.

Default bid:
Enter any number here, we are going to change it later.

Budget:
Enter your daily budget.

Ad Extensions:
Ad extensions, otherwise known as sitelinks, are a great way to encourage more clicks to your site. Enter as many relevant entries as you can, if you have an office address and phone number, use it.

Schedule:
If you are only open during certain business hours, enter the hours you want to be running ads here. For some businesses, it's okay to run your campaign 24x7, because some customers will send an online enquiry if they arrive at your website outside of business hours. If you are selling something like a local food, such as a pizza shop, you might want to restrict your campaigns to only run during your opening hours.

Ad delivery:
Choose 'Rotate indefinitely. Show lower performing ads more evenly with higher performing ads, and do not optimize'.

Why would you want to choose this you might wonder? You want to run your ads evenly, so you have reliable data when you review your ads, and can objectively see which ads are performing better for your goals.

You can leave the rest of settings for now, hit 'save and continue', and you're good to go with setting up the rest of your campaign.

Optimization tips for tweaking your campaign for better profit.

I've touched on a handful of secrets of successful pay-per-click campaigns, but I'm going to wrap up this special bonus chapter with the most important habit for pay-per-click success.

Review your campaign regularly.

Leaving an AdWords campaign running without keeping your head around the performance is like leaving a freight-train running without a driver.

Regularly reviewing your ad performance, ad group performance, keyword performance and cost-per-click will allow you to back the winning horses of your campaign, and cut swiftly cut the losers.

Fortunately, the AdWords platform offers endless opportunities for deep insights into the performance of your campaign.

As a starting point, I've listed below some example areas in your campaign to look over. Review the below areas and optimize your campaign for better results.

- Ad group performance. Review click-through-rates, cost-per-click, and cost-per-conversion. Allocate more funds from your campaign to winning ad groups, and decrease funds or pause losing ad groups if you see any obvious trends.

- Ad performance. Look for winning ads with higher click-through-rates, lower cost-per-clicks, and lower cost-per-conversion. Pause losing ads, and create new ads to split-test based on your winners. Progressively build up new ads with higher click-through-rates into your campaign over time.

- Keyword performance. Review which keywords are running at a higher cost, which keywords have low quality scores, and see if you can pause any overly budget-draining keywords with low conversions.

That wraps up the special bonus chapter on AdWords.

If you want to delve deeper into the pay-per-click rabbit-hole, the below resources are a great starting point for anyone starting out with pay-per-click advertising.

Ultimate Guide to Google AdWords - Perry Marshall

The ultimate guide to Google Adwords by Perry Marshall is often the starting point for many professionals starting out with PPC. Offers a great overview of AdWords and delves into the 'inner game' of successful AdWords campaigns. Great for beginners, but for advanced techniques check out some of the resources below.

Advanced Google AdWords - Brad Geddes

If you want to be a pay-per-click guru, then look no further than this fantastic guide to advanced AdWords management, for agencies and business owners running their own campaigns. Brad Geddes' magnum opus on advanced AdWords pay-per-click advertising has been the secret treasure of many-a-successful pay-per-click consultant's career. Readily available on Amazon.com

PPC Hero
http://www.ppchero.com/

PPC Hero is loaded with free advice on the latest AdWords tricks and tips, but also covering fundamental pay-per-click methods that never change. Updated regularly.

Inside AdWords
http://adwords.blogspot.com.au/

Google's official blog for AdWords. Great for the latest AdWords news direct from the horses mouth.

Certified Knowledge
http://certifiedknowledge.org/blog/

The Certified Knowledge Blog by Brad Geddes offers the latest AdWords news and advice by one of the world's leading authorities on advanced AdWords advertising.

Final thoughts

You could spend decades reading all the different techniques for SEO and never get anywhere. After years of learning what works and what doesn't, I've presented the most effective tactics for SEO, kept this book up-to-date in the face of constant Google changes, to help readers quickly and effectively become skilled at SEO at a professional level.

The advice in this book is more than enough to get started in SEO successfully and increase the rankings, traffic and sales for your site...

But don't forget why we learn SEO in the first place.

The details are important, but don't get bogged down in them.

It's painfully easy to get lost in the endless sea of information on SEO and never make any progress with your projects or goals.

What matters is you optimize your site well enough to beat your competitors, make more sales, and grow your business.

These strategies work for my projects, they work for my clients and they will work for you. If your site shows stronger signals to Google than your competitors, you will beat them in the rankings.

Most importantly, have fun with it.

--

Thanks for reading, I hope you enjoyed this book. If you would like me to write more books on growing your business online, please put up some stars and a review to support the book.

- Adam Clarke

40802248R00091

Made in the USA
Lexington, KY
18 April 2015